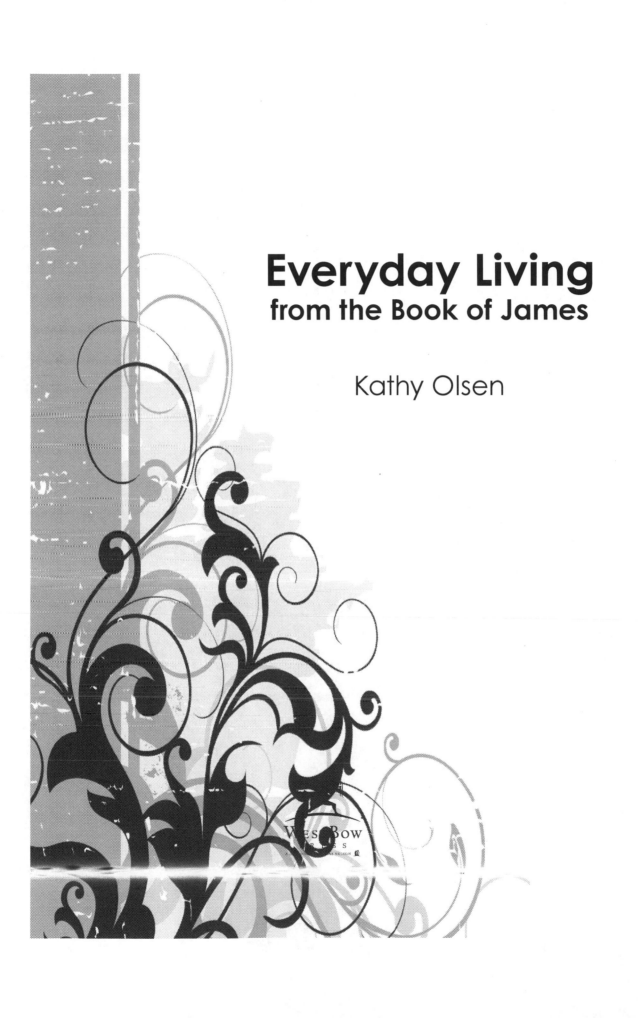

Everyday Living
from the Book of James

Kathy Olsen

WestBow
PRESS
A DIVISION OF THOMAS NELSON & ZONDERVAN

WestBow Press books may be ordered through booksellers or by contacting:

WestBow Press
A Division of Thomas Nelson
1663 Liberty Drive
Bloomington, IN 47403
www.westbowpress.com
1-(866) 928-1240

Because of the dynamic nature of the Internet, any web addresses or links contained in this book may have changed since publication and may no longer be valid. The views expressed in this work are solely those of the author and do not necessarily reflect the views of the publisher, and the publisher hereby disclaims any responsibility for them.

Any people depicted in stock imagery provided by Thinkstock are models, and such images are being used for illustrative purposes only.

Certain stock imagery © Thinkstock.

ISBN: 978-1-4497-1409-3 (sc)
ISBN: 978-1-4497-1408-6 (e)

Library of Congress Control Number: 2011925110

Printed in the United States of America

WestBow Press rev. date: 03/15/2011

Contents

Introduction to Everyday Living from the Book of James

Welcome to our journey through the book of James. Are you excited and ready to learn some practical "how-to's" for living a life that is pleasing to God? You can count on the fact that as you study His word, God will challenge you, stretch you, encourage you and grow you spiritually.

God's word excites me; it always has, which is why this study exists—to excite you about God and His word in perhaps new and different ways ultimately drawing you ever-closer to Him. Having a passion for women and God's word, I have spent many years connecting the two together through teaching bible studies, leading small groups and mentoring women in one-on-one relationships. This passion from God led me to a calling by God several years ago as the Women's Ministry Leader at my home church, Valley Real Life in Spokane Valley, Washington.

In my many years of walking with God, His word has never disappointed me--oh, it has challenged me, angered me, convicted me, encouraged and directed me, but it has never let me down! I have found His word to be practical as well as applicable in my day-to-day life. Perhaps that is why God drew me to a study in the book of James.

Before we dive into our study, it's important to spend a bit of time identifying and learning about the author of the book of James. The first James who comes to mind as a possible author is the apostle James, John's brother and Zebedee's son. This James, however, was put to death by King Herod in AD 44 (see Acts 12:2 NIV), and most scholars believe this book to have been written around AD 50. If the AD 50 dating is correct, this letter would be the earliest of the New Testament writings with the possible exception of Galatians.

Most scholars accept James, the brother of Jesus (not the apostle James) as the author of this New Testament letter. There are a number of things we can learn about him from Scripture.

Matthew 13:55 tells us that Jesus had four brothers, James, Joses, Simon and Judas (also called Jude). He also had sisters, although we don't know how many. Following Jesus, James was most likely the oldest brother since his name is listed first among his siblings. During the life and ministry of Jesus, James did not accept either Jesus' claims or his authority; however, after the resurrection of Jesus, it was a whole new ball game. According to 1 Corinthians 15, after Jesus was raised on the third day, he appeared to Peter, to the apostles, to more than 500 believers and finally to James. From that point on, James was convinced that Jesus was who He claimed to be!

James went on to become one of the leaders of the church in Jerusalem. In his letter to the Galatians, Paul described James as one of the "pillars" of the church (Galatians 1:19, 2:9). James also presided at the first Council of Jerusalem (Acts 15) establishing guidelines for Gentile (non-Jewish) believers for more harmonious Christian fellowship with their Jewish brothers and sisters. James became so well known that Jude (Jude 1:1) identified himself simply as "a brother of James." James died about A.D. 62 as a martyr by stoning at the instigation of the high priest Ananus.

The recipients of James' letter are identified in James 1:1 as "the twelve tribes scattered among the nations." The term "twelve tribes" refers to Jewish Christians descending from the original twelve tribes of Israel, but why were the Jewish Christians "scattered?"

Fear and persecution are huge motivators as to why someone might choose to pack up and leave family, friends and home. After the persecution and stoning of Stephen in Jerusalem by the Jewish ruling council known as the Sanhedrin (Acts 8:1-3), it's easy to see how fear might have begun to spread among believers. Concern that what happened to Stephen may happen to them as well perhaps led them to "scatter among the nations." This would explain why James refers to trials and oppression in his letter, and as the leader of the Jerusalem church, his desire would have been to encourage and instruct his scattered flock who were facing difficulties.

The book of James is similar to the book of Proverbs in that both are considered to be types of wisdom literature. To understand something about wisdom literature, perhaps we need to identify what biblical wisdom looks like: It is the art of successful living; of knowing how to form the correct plan to gain the desired results through the lens and filter of the word and ways of God.

Biblical wisdom is both spiritual and practical and touches all areas of life. It takes insights learned about God's nature and character from his word and applies it to everyday life. Another way to say it might be, "Godly head knowledge with feet." James teaches about:

- trials and temptations
- the testing of our faith
- favoritism
- faith and actions
- the tongue
- wisdom
- quarrels
- spiritual unfaithfulness
- pride
- slander
- boasting
- patience in suffering
- prayer

As you can see, this book is chock-full of practical teachings and applications for living. Before we get started, though, let's talk about how you can gain the maximum benefit from this study over the next several weeks.

The study guide consists of 10 lessons that are completed on a weekly basis. Each lesson has five individual day's worth of study. The intent and design is to digest God's word slowly, daily rather than gorging yourself all in one sitting. When we "gorge," we lose the ability to *taste and see that the Lord is good*" (Psalm 34:8a) because we are scanning, skimming and skipping through the lesson in order to get it done before the deadline. <u>Remember that the rate of your investment will affect the rate of your return!</u>

Because "tasting and seeing" take time, it might be helpful to set apart a specific time each day, if possible, to work on your study so that you have time to ponder a scripture verse or question and answer with God without feeling rushed or hurried. Unless otherwise noted, all scripture references will be taken from the New International Version (NIV) translation of the Bible.

Never forget to keep your focus on the ultimate goal of this study: To draw you closer to God through knowledge of His word.

So what are we waiting for..............LET'S GET STARTED!

Lesson 1

James 1:1-12

Read James 1:2-12 asking God for the guidance of His Holy Spirit.

"Consider it pure joy, my brothers, whenever you face trials of many kinds..."

Are you kidding me? Do "joy" and "trials" really belong in the same sentence? How can they possibly co-exist? Is there truly a way to experience joy when your life seems to be falling apart around you?

Let's focus on James 1:2-3. Dictionary.com defines a trial as "an affliction or trouble; a trying, distressing or annoying thing or person."

In the context of these verses, trials are seen as difficulties that come from the outside; they are events or circumstances that "happen" to us in which we have absolutely no control over.

- Share the most recent trial/test you've experienced or are currently going through.

  _____

  _____

- How do you normally view and handle your personal trials?

  _____

  _____

Like most of us, we couldn't possibly say that trials in life make us happy because they don't! We do not like problems creeping into the order and routine of our daily lives, but if James says to consider it "pure joy" whenever we face trials, there must be more to joy than a fleeting feeling of elation that we call "happiness."

In looking at the following verses, where do tests/trials come from and what are some of the reasons?

- Isaiah 48:10-11 _____

- Exodus 20:20 _____

- Psalm 139:23-24 _____

- Hebrews 11:17-19_____

- Exodus 16:4 _____

From James 1:3, what does James have to say about the purpose of trials?

_____

_____

Read 1 Peter 1:6-7. What does Peter say about:

Trials: _____

Faith: _____

- From the context of all the previous verses, how can we find joy in the midst of our trials and how does that differ from happiness?

_____

_____

In God's sight, our faith is of greater worth than gold. Wow! How precious our faith is to God! The writer of Hebrews takes his readers through an historical overview of many Old Testament heroes who operated in faith. For this reason, Hebrews 11 has fondly become known as the "Hall of Faith."

*Take some time to prayerfully read Hebrews 11 about these faithful men and women who were called to walk in faith **JUST LIKE US!** Remember, walking in faith does not imply that there is no fear involved, but that surpassing any fear is a willful choice to walk in the promises of God.*

- According to vs. 1-2 of Hebrews 11, why were these Old Testament heroes commended?

_____

- Summarize Hebrews 11:6 in your own words. _____

_____

_____

Scripture makes it clear that our faith is of utmost importance to God. Faith is the "key" that opens the "door" to a relationship with God, our Father. However, we must always remember that the "door" is none other than Jesus Christ.

"I am the way, the truth and the life. No one comes to the father except through me." John 14:6

How has God spoken to you in today's study? _____

_____

We learned yesterday that problems can be more than headaches in life and pains in our...backsides; they are actually from God and are designed to test and grow our faith in Him. We can now view trials in our lives from a whole new perspective.

Begin this time asking God's guidance as you re-read James 1:3 and vs. 12

Perseverance is the idea of "staying on a charted course <u>in spite of</u> opposition." The logical conclusion, then, would have to be that where there is no opposition, there can be no perseverance, right?

Let's look at a great example of perseverance in the life of Moses in Hebrews 11:23-27.

- In these few short verses, list some of the opposition Moses faced.

  _____

List any additional opposition Moses faced from the following verses:

- Exodus 3:11, 4:1,10,13 _____

- Exodus 14:1-4 _____

- Exodus 14:10-12 _____

- Exodus 17:1-4 _____

- Exodus 17:8-9 _____

- Exodus 18:13-18 _____

- Exodus 32:1-4 _____

- Numbers 12:1-2 _____

Moses had to face his fears: The Egyptian government, those he was called to lead (Israelites), foreign enemies, physical weariness, and even opposition from his own brother and sister (Aaron & Miriam).

- In Hebrews 11:26, to what was Moses was looking ahead? _____

- From Hebrews 10:35-36, why are we encouraged not to "throw away our confidence" or let go of our faith?

  _____

  _____

What are some of the things God has promised?

- John 3:16 _____

- 1 Corinthians 10:13 _____

- James 1:12 _____

For what are we rewarded?

- 2 Samuel 22:25 _____

- 2 Chronicles 15:7 _____

- Psalm 19:7-11 _____

- Jeremiah 17:10 _____

- Matthew 5:11-12 _____

- Hebrews 11:6 _____

- What was the secret to Moses perseverance? (Hebrews 11:27)

  _____

- How can we "see" someone or something that is invisible? _____

  _____

Read Hebrews 12:1-4

- Who are we to fix our eyes on? _____

- List some of the reasons why we <u>must</u> fix our eyes on Jesus? _____

  _____

*Focusing on Jesus helps us keep our own struggles in perspective, doesn't it? While we don't ever want to minimize the personal difficulties each of us faces in our lives, none of us have had to face torture and death as Jesus did, would you agree? And yet, He told his followers in John16:33: "**I have told you these things so that in me you may have peace. In this world, you <u>will</u> have trouble. But take heart! I have overcome the world!**" Amen!*

- Summarize in your own words the encouragement we receive from the Apostle Paul in 2 Corinthians 4:16-18 _____

_____

_____

How has God spoken to you in today's lesson? _____

_____

Below is a poem that was found many years ago. These words from an unknown author can keep you persevering when you want to quit. Ironically, the title of the poem is just that, "DON'T QUIT."

When things go wrong, as they sometimes will,
When the road you're trudging seems all uphill,
When the funds are low and the debts are high,
And you want to smile, but you have to sigh,
When care is pressing you down a bit,
Rest, if you must, but don't you quit.
Life is queer with its twists and turns,
As every one of us sometimes learns,
And many a failure turns about,
When he might have won had he stuck it out;
Don't give up though the pace seems slow—
You may succeed with another blow.
Success is failure turned inside out—
The silver tint of the clouds of doubt,
And you never can tell how close you are,
It may be near when it seems so far,
So stick to the fight when you're hardest hit—
It's when things seem worst that you
MUST NOT QUIT!

Yesterday, we saw that perseverance has a definite purpose. Do you remember the definition of perseverance? Write it out in the margin to help remind you. Perseverance tests, refines and grows our faith. Today we're going to see that there is also an end result to perseverance.

Read James 1:4

- According to James, what is the "work" that perseverance accomplishes?

_____

So what exactly is spiritual maturity? Besides that, how do we get it, and what are some of the obstacles that stand in our way?

<u>WHAT IS SPIRITUAL MATURITY?</u>

Read Hebrews 5:11-14

The spiritually mature:

1. Have been acquainted with the ***teaching about righteousness***.

2. ***Constantly live on solid food.***

3. ***Have trained themselves to distinguish good from evil.***

1. **TEACHING ABOUT RIGHTEOUSNESS**

   Let's go back to the beginning to Abraham, the "Father of Righteousness".

   Read Romans 4:18-22

   - Why was Abraham credited with righteousness? _____

   - What was God's promise to Abraham? (Genesis 15:1-6) _____

   - How did Abraham show his belief? (Hebrews 11:17-19) _____

   _____

   Read Romans 4:23-25 & 6:15-18

   - How are we credited with righteousness?_____

   - How do we show our belief? _____

   - What do you now believe is the "teaching about righteousness? _____

   _____

God set us free from slavery to sin (even though we didn't even know we were slaves), in order to allow us to willingly choose to become a slave to obedience (to God) which leads to righteousness.

2. **CONSTANTLY LIVE ON SOLID FOOD**

    What would living on solid food look like from the following verses?

    Acts 17:10-11 _____

    Psalm 1:1&2 _____

    Hebrews 4:12&13 _____

    What do you now believe "constantly living on solid" food looks like?

    _____

    What does your life consist of, milk or solid food?

    _____

3. **TRAINED THEMSELVES TO DISTINGUISH GOOD FROM EVIL**

    Good from evil can also be described as truth from lies. Where does truth come from?

    John 14:6 _____

    John 16:13 _____

    John 17:17 _____

    Where do lies come from?

    John 8:44-47 _____

    How can you train yourself to distinguish truth from lies? _____

    _____

HOW DO WE GET SPIRITUAL MATURITY?

Who's better than the Apostle Paul to show us his daily spiritual regimen for maturity.

Read Philippians 3:12-16 and list all the action phrases you find.

_____

In order to understand what Paul was seeking to "take hold of," we need to back up a bit.

Paul had an impressive family history, educational excellence and impressive personal credentials, and yet in coming to know Jesus Christ he considered them as loss.

Let's read Philippians 3:7-11 together.

- Why did Paul consider his credentials as loss? _____

   _____

- What was he trying to "take hold of?" _____

   _____

- Reread Philippians 3:15. On what "things" are the spiritually mature to take a particular view? _____

- Where do you see yourself on the maturity scale?

A baby on milk   **Milk & solid food**   **Spiritually Mature**

Perhaps you don't like where you placed yourself on the above scale. Well then, let's look at some of the things that may be holding you back in your maturing process.

WHAT ARE SOME OF THE OBSTACLES IN REACHING SPIRITUAL MATURITY?

Read Luke 8:4-8

Jesus often spoke to his listeners in parables. A "parable" is really just an earthly story with a heavenly meaning–a teaching with word pictures. In this instance, Jesus goes further with his disciples and explains the meaning of the parable to them.

Read Luke 8:11-15 and answer the following:

Parable	Jesus' Meaning
Seed	_____
Path	_____
Rock	_____
Thorns	_____
Good soil	_____

So, what holds you back in your maturing process? _____

_____

Have you noticed a theme over the past 3 days? Yep, you guessed it. It's

P – E – R – S – E – V – E – R – A – N – C – E

What has God shown you in today's lesson? _____

_____

_____

I'm so glad you're still with us as we head into Day 4. Remember, Satan is going to try to distract and discourage you in any way he can in your personal study time. Keep in mind that the only reason he'll do this is because he doesn't want you to know God's truth! (Remember, he's the "Father of Lies.") So persevere, ladies, as we dig into today's text.

Read James 1:5-8

We know a mature Christian lacks nothing (vs. 4), but since most of us are still in the maturing process, James suggests a possible lack we may still have--wisdom. The wisdom James is speaking of here refers to an understanding of the ways of God and a willingness to act according to those ways. Basically, it's taking Godly knowledge and living it out in our everyday lives.

-   Read Proverbs 2:1-9 and list some of the actions we must take in order to attain wisdom.

    _____

-   Contrast this to James 1:5. What action is necessary from us here? _____

-   Do you see this as a contradiction of scripture? Please explain. _____

    _____

Since wisdom is "living out" the knowledge and understanding we have of God's ways, simply "asking" is not some magic pill we take in order to suddenly have wisdom.

So then, what exactly are we asking for? We are asking God for the understanding of His ways and the ability and commitment to live out His ways.

-   Fill in what else verse 5 has to say. "....God, who gives _____ to

    all _____ _____ _____, and it will be given to him."

-   How do these promises encourage you? _____

    _____

Re-read Proverbs 2:1-9 again this time listing some of the benefits of wisdom.

_____

_____

Wisdom is kind of the carrot being dangled in front of us, isn't it? It's as if God is saying, "Look what I have for you. As you keep persevering in your trials, know that your faith is growing, and you're gaining an understanding of who I am and knowing my ways which will bring you wisdom." There is, however, a stipulation in our "asking" as we see in James 1:6.

- What is the stipulation? _____

- Why do you think James uses the example of a wave of the sea and the wind?

   _____

   _____

At first glance, verse 7 seems a bit harsh, doesn't it? When we ask, we <u>must believe</u> and have <u>no doubt</u>, or we won't receive anything from God. Let's break it down and try to make sense of the actual meaning from these verses.

*The Greek phrase for "must believe" can more accurately be translated as "in faith." We are learning that faith is active; therefore, "stepping out" in faith would indicate no hesitation of action. So, with that in mind, let's look at the beginning of verse 6 again in this way; but when he asks **in faith without hesitating**...it will be given to him.*

Of course, you may have some internal battle with doubt in a particular situation, but this internal struggle does not cause you to hesitate in your step of active faith. Maybe verses 7 & 8 will become a little clearer now. Let's read them together.

- What do you think is meant by the term "double-minded"? _____

   _____

- Read Matthew 7:17-18, 21 and summarize what Jesus is saying. _____

   _____

- Does this change or clarify your previous definition of "double-minded"?

   _____

A "double-minded" person has a divided heart that shows up through divided loyalties and commitment which leads to an instability of purpose. Can you see how this type of person should not expect a positive answer from God when asking? Basically, God is waiting for that person to make up his mind.

A mother once used the analogy of a picket fence with her daughters during their teen years saying:

"You have a picket fence up your rear end from sitting on the fence. You have too much of the world in you to enjoy God and too much of God in you to enjoy the world. At some point, you're gonna have to get off the fence."

- How about you? Are you on that fence? _____

- Do you have a divided heart in any way? _____

_____

How has God spoken to you in today's study? _____

_____

_____

Let's dive right into our final section of verses concluding the last day of our study in Lesson 1.

Read James 1:9-11

Are you scratching your head and wondering why James stuck these verses in here? At first glance, it sure seems to be out of place, doesn't it? Maybe not though...

Our theme this week has been trials: having trials with joy, persevering in trials and seeking wisdom in our trials. So if we keep with this same theme in regards to riches and poverty (humble circumstances), they too can present trials in our lives.

- From Proverbs 30:8-9, how can both riches and poverty be seen as trials?

_____

_____

Poverty and wealth can be very subjective terms based on the glasses you're looking through. We can always find someone richer than us both economically and materially and feel we are poor by comparison. Please understand there is no attempt to minimize the fact that there are many people who are truly living in economic poverty; we also don't want to confuse true poverty with those who are suffering financially simply because they are mismanaging their money.

The concept James keeps trying to get across is one of attitude. He started out by telling us to "count it all joy" when you face trials (vs. 2), then he goes on to tell us why (vs. 3); finally, in verses 9 & 10 he tells us to "take pride" in our circumstances whether rich or poor. The Greek term "to take pride in" can be used to speak of boasting or glorying in someone or something. This "glorying" in our circumstances, again, has to do with attitude.

- What do you think James means by the following?

  "The brother in humble circumstances should take pride in his high position."

  _____

  "The one who is rich should take pride in his low position." _____

  _____

James encourages us to see our life experiences from God's perspective rather than those of the world.

In what way do the below verses turn our world views upside down?

- Matthew 23:11-12 _____

- Mark 9:33-35 _____

- 2 Corinthians 12:9-10 _____

- 1 Corinthians 3:18-19a _____

God does not view our circumstances in the same way we do. By humbling ourselves, we are exalted by God; placing ourselves last makes us first in God's eyes; when we are weak, God sees us as strong; the world's wisdom is seen as foolishness by God.

Although, we can easily become impressed by people with riches and look down upon those we see as poor, <u>GOD DOES NOT.</u>

- (Personal reflection) Do you see those with riches as greater and those without as lesser? Or, do you, perhaps, see those with wealth as "less than" spiritually?

- How can we become dependent on God in the below areas?

  Poverty _____

  Riches _____

Remember, God desires to use any and all of our life experiences and circumstances to draw us closer to him.

Poverty can cause us to depend on God to meet our physical needs. As he meets those needs, we draw closer to him (our high position). The wealthy, however, don't "need" God to meet their physical needs and can easily lose sight of their spiritual need for God causing them to have a "low position."

- What perspective and warning do we gain from 1 Timothy 6:7-10?

_____

_____

Focus on verses 10b & 11 in James 1.

- What point do you think James is trying to make? _____

_____

- Why do you think James is singling out the one who is rich in this passage?

_____

Since we know that everyone (rich and poor alike) will "pass away like a wild flower" (that is, face death), James is challenging the rich person to keep their wealth in perspective - it's fleeting, as is their life.

Finish up by reading Isaiah 40:6-8

- What are we promised does last forever?_____

How has God spoken to you in today's lesson? _____

_____

Lesson 2

James 1:13-18

We're shifting gears this week from trials to temptations; although, they are closely linked. During our times of trials and testing is when we will most often experience our strongest temptations. The lines can easily become blurred between the two, and we can begin to believe God is behind both our trials and our temptations. Our natural response is to then ask God, "Why is this happening to me?"

Read James 1:13 and fill in the below:

For God _____ _____ _____ by evil, nor does he _____ anyone.

Let's explore why God cannot be tempted by evil.

Read Hebrews 5:14 . What are we being trained to distinguish? _____

According to Romans 12:9, what attitude are we to have towards good and evil?

_____

What do the following verses say about good and evil?

- Mark 10:18 _____

- Psalm 34:8 _____

- Matthew 6:13 _____

- Isaiah 5:20 _____

Based on the above verses, why can't God be tempted by evil?

_____

Evil is the complete absence of good, and because God is inherently good, he cannot be tempted by evil nor can he tempt anyone else towards evil. Satan is the author of evil, and he is the one who tempts us to sin.

In looking up the dictionary definition for "evil," we come across some synonyms (similar words) for evil: sinful, iniquitous, depraved, vicious, corrupt, vile, nefarious, destructive, wicked. Wow! The baddest of the bad, right? These are things like child pornography, murder, sexual deviations and the like. I think you'll find it interesting to see the things that God includes in his definition of "evil."

Read Romans 1:28-32 along with Colossians 3:5-9

- List some of the things that God considers to be evil. _____

- List any that may have surprised you from this list. _____

Prayerfully ask God to show you if and how you struggle in any of these particular areas. I've left room below each for you to write your own personal notes and comments.

Envy - <u>a feeling of discontent</u> or covetousness with regard to another's advantages, success, possessions, etc.

Strife - a vigorous or bitter conflict; a quarrel, struggle or clash; <u>competition or rivalry</u>

Gossip - idle talk or rumor especially about the personal or private affairs of others (often disguised as "pray for so-and-so").

Slander - a malicious, false, and defamatory statement or report. (What about twisting the truth? Doesn't that make it false?)

Greed - excessive desire especially for wealth or possessions.

Anger - wrath; ire.

Malice - desire to inflict injury, harm, or suffering on another, either because of a hostile impulse or out of deep-seated meanness. (Ever wanted to get even????)

James 5:16 says to "confess your sins to each other and pray for each other so that you may be healed."

- (Personal) Please share honestly with your group about one of these areas you are currently struggling with and ask for prayer and accountability.

How has God spoken to you in today's lesson? _____

*Yesterday we looked at where evil comes from and God's view towards evil; today we are going to see how we can be enticed towards evil. **Let's read James 1:14** together: "...but each one is tempted when, by his own evil desire, he is dragged away and enticed."*

The NASB uses the term "lust" in place of "evil desire." Lust is "a passionate or overmastering desire or craving." If we used this definition in place of "evil desire" in vs. 14, it would sound something like this: "...but each one is tempted when, by his own passionate or overmastering desire or craving , he is dragged away and enticed." Can you relate at all? The implication here is that we all have within us our own individual desires and cravings; they don't come from outside us; they live within us.

Let's go back... way back to the beginning in the book of Genesis to look at the origination of lust, temptation and evil.

Please read Genesis 2:15-17 & 3:1-13.

- What were God's instructions to Adam? _____

  _____

- What did Eve add to God's instructions? _____

- How did the serpent (Satan) tempt them by further changing God's instructions?

  _____

  _____

- What was the core of Adam and Eve's lust? _____

  _____

- How did Eve rationalize her lust? _____

  _____

- How have you rationalized your own desires and cravings? _____

  _____

  _____

*Have you ever noticed how the minute something becomes off limits or forbidden, out bubbles the desire or craving for that very thing? Now why is that? Adam and Eve had everything they could possibly want **except** for one little thing, and that one little thing is exactly what Satan capitalized on when tempting Eve. The lust for the forbidden came from within Eve, and Satan did the rest. James 1:14 says that by our own evil desire, we are "dragged away and enticed."*

The idea of being dragged away suggests that it is something that happens to us against our will (i.e. being dragged kicking and screaming). However, in the context of this verse, it is more appropriately used in the figurative sense of being drawn out or away by some desire. A good example of this is in fishing: You use bait to attract or lure a fish in order to hook it and catch it.

Let's look at another example in 2 Timothy 2:24-26.

- Who sets the trap? _____

- What is our captivity?_____

- How can we escape the trap?_____

Knowing God's truth keeps us in our right mind ("come to our senses"), so to speak, which then allows us to escape from the trap of Satan's lies.

- If we look back to the account in Genesis in the Garden of Eden, how was Eve dragged away and enticed?

  _____

- In this picture of being "dragged away," what do you think Eve was being dragged away from?

  _____

Have you noticed the order of the sequence? Our lust leads us to first be dragged away and then enticed, not the other way around.

- Why do you think we have to be dragged away before we can be enticed?

  _____

  _____

- How do you personally guard against being dragged away? _____

  _____

Lust drags a person away from God's right path (truth), luring us with false promises of an immediate fulfillment of pleasure. This constitutes the true nature of temptation, capturing both temptation's attractiveness and destructiveness.

How has God spoken to you in today's lesson? _____

_____

_____

In James 1:15, James paints a word picture of the cycle of life (from conception to birth and ultimately death) to try and make a point regarding how sin enters our lives and the eventual result of our sin. In order to fully understand the results of sin, it's important that we look at sin from God's perspective rather than our own.

The principle New Testament term for sin is "hamartia." In classical Greek it is used for missing a target or taking a wrong road. It is the general New Testament term for sin as concrete wrongdoing, the violation of God's law (also seen as contempt for God's law). The inner motivation towards sin is seen as rebellion against God, an action in breach of relationship. Since God is all about relationship, and the heart is at the center of every intimate relationship, sin can also be expressed as "missing or acting against the heart of God."

Read Matthew 15:7-20

In this passage, Jesus was addressing the Pharisees and teachers of the law (the religious leaders of Jesus' day).

- Why did Jesus call the religious leaders hypocrites? _____
  _____

- Explain the meaning of the parable Jesus used in vs. 10 & 11: _____
  _____

Read and summarize 1 Samuel 16:7 and Psalm 51:16-17: _____
_____

How about you? Do you find yourself more concerned with how others see you or about what God sees in your heart?
_____
_____

Do you see how easy it could be to fake our Christian walk? Because others see what's on the outside (what we want them to see), rebellion, pride, lust, envy or a whole host of other things could be going on in our hearts and no one else would know, right? Except for God, that is.

So let's go back now and review James 1:14 and add vs. 15.

- What do you think James means when he says, "After desire has conceived...?"
  _____

One of the best examples regarding this idea of desire conceiving is from the words to a song by Casting Crowns called "Slow Fade."

Be careful little eyes what you see
It's the second glance that ties your hands as darkness pulls the strings.
Be careful little feet where you go
For it's the little feet behind you that are sure to follow.
Be careful little ears what you hear
When flattery leads to compromise, the end is always near.
Be careful little lips what you say
For empty words and promises lead broken hearts astray.
It's a slow fade when you give yourself away.
It's a slow fade when black and white have turned to gray.
Thoughts invade, choices are made, a price will be paid when you give yourself away.
People never crumble in a day.

Desire causes us to justify and rationalize that which we want to do but know is wrong before God. ..."when black and white have turned to gray."

James says that "after desire has conceived, it gives birth to sin; and sin, when it is full-grown, gives birth to death." ..."Thoughts invade, choices are made, a price will be paid when you give yourself away."

- What is the ultimate result or price paid for our sin? _____

The dictionary defines death as "the act of dying; the end of life; the total and permanent cessation of all the vital functions of an organism."

But death happens to all of us eventually, right? So if that's the case, there must be more to this idea of death coming as a result of sin. Well then, let's go back to our good friends Adam and Eve for some insight.

Please read Genesis 2:9,16-17

- What were the two trees in the middle of the garden? _____

- From which of the two trees were they free to eat? _____

God told Adam and Eve they could eat freely from the tree of life; God's design has always been for us to live eternally in relationship with Him.

- What did God say would happen if Adam and Eve ate from the tree of the knowledge of good and evil?

  _____

- Look back again at the dictionary definition of death. In eating from the tree, their physical life didn't come to an end, did it? So what did happen?

  (Read Genesis 3:7-8)

  _____

- How did their sin affect their relationship with God? _____

  _____

- How has your sin affected your relationship with God either now or in the past?

  _____

Because of their sin, Adam and Eve separated themselves from God (hid from Him); there was a death of relationship. Each and every time we willfully sin, our relationship with God is affected. We pull away in guilt and shame (coming from Satan), and we hide. However, we are promised in 1 John 1:9 that "If we confess our sins to him, He is faithful and just to forgive us and to cleanse us from every wrong." A restoration of relationship with God happens as a result of this act of confession on our part and His forgiveness.

When the time comes, our physical bodies will cease to exist (death by the world's terminology). However, because we are spiritual creatures, we will continue to live eternally within God's purpose and design; it will either be in eternal relationship with Him or in eternal separation from Him.

How has God spoken to you in today's lesson? _____

_____

In reading James 1:16-17, verse 16 starts out by saying, "Do not be deceived, my dear brothers." About what? In order to understand his warning, we have to look back and then forward. James has been talking about evil and temptation and where they come from; he then moves forward and begins talking about where "good and perfect gifts" originate--from the Father of the heavenly lights.

James points out the stark contrast between the insidious nature of evil desire and God's nature; God's gifts are good, not evil. Temptation (an evil force which leads to sin and death) has its source in human desire while good gifts have God as their source.

- Without looking in a dictionary, define "good" in your own words.

  _____

- By what standards do you judge something to be either "good" or "bad"?
  (i.e. experience, feelings, scripture, personal belief)

  _____

- What do the following verses say about good?

  Nehemiah 9:20 _____

  Psalm 25:8 _____

  Psalm 84:11 _____

  Micah 6:8 _____

  John 10:11 _____

  John 16:7 _____

*Since God is good, He **cannot** be bad; goodness is the essence of His nature and character. How He acts, what He allows, and which gifts He gives are all based out of His goodness.*

- Summarize Matthew 7:9-11 _____

  _____

Let's take this analogy of a parent/child a bit further. Suppose you have a 3-year-old child who begins pitching fits every night at dinnertime because he doesn't want to eat dinner but wants cookies instead; he cries and pleads and throws a tantrum trying to get what he wants. He sees your denial of his desires as "bad" and mean.

You love your child and want the very best for him and hate to see him unhappy.

- What would you do? Why? _____

_____

I certainly hope that we can all agree that it would not be in his best interest to give him cookies instead of dinner every night, right? From your position as a parent, you know that his body needs a balance of foods for him to be healthy physically and emotionally and that, even though he wants the cookies, his perspective is limited by his immaturity, his selfish desires and his lack of understanding of the long-term consequences. (Sound like anyone we know?)

- Summarize Luke 18:19 and Isaiah 55:8. _____

_____

*It's all a matter of perspective, isn't it? We don't see the bigger picture as God does. Since we cannot see from God's perspective, we must rely in faith on the fact that God is good. While His ways and knowledge are beyond our understanding, He is **on our side** and is working for our ultimate spiritual good in each and every situation that comes our way in life.*

James goes on to say in verse 17 that we can also rest in the fact that God never changes. He won't send good gifts one day and then something bad the next just because He is cranky, tired or frustrated with us.

- What does Hebrews 13:8 say about this? _____

- How does this truth impact you? _____

_____

- How can this truth be applied in a practical way in your everyday life?

_____

_____

How has God spoken to you in today's lesson? _____

_____

Most of the focus this week has been on our evil desires along with Satan's temptations which lead to sin-- remember that sin equals spiritual death or separation from God. So James now switches gear in order to offer us some much-needed hope. This struggle regarding our evil desires vs. God's desires is shared by the apostle Paul. Comforting to know, isn't it?

- Read Paul's words in Romans 7:18-23 and summarize his struggle. _____

_____

- Where did Paul's hope come from? (Romans 7:24-25) _____

Read James 1:18, and we'll focus on three key points: word of truth, birth and firstfruits.

1. Word of Truth:

    - What do you learn about the "word" in John 1:1-4,14? _____

    _____

    - In John 18:38, Pilate asked Jesus, "What is truth?" How would you answer that from the following scriptures:

    John 8:31&32 _____

    John 14:6 _____

    John 16:13 _____

    John 17:_____

2. Birth: In John 3:3-8, Jesus explained birth, or being "born again," to Nicodemus. What do you think Jesus meant when he said, "...no one can see the kingdom of God unless he is born again?"

    _____

3. Firstfruits: This term is used often as a designator of believers in the New Testament; in the Old Testament, it's referenced in several different ways.

- ***First ripening of a harvest or first offspring of an animal***

    Exodus 23:16, 19 _____

    Leviticus 27:26 _____

- ***Firstborn among males***

    Exodus 34:19 _____

- ***Israel as God's firstborn or chosen people***

    Exodus 4:22 _____

    Deuteronomy 7:6 _____

    Jeremiah 2:3 _____

The first ripening of the harvest or first offspring of an animal was offered to God in acknowledgement that He owns everything. The firstfruits were considered sacred, set apart for God. The nation of Israel was also considered as God's firstborn or firstfruit spiritually. Likewise, we, as New Testament believers, are set apart as God's special people for His purpose and design.

- From your study of the above regarding the word of Truth, birth and firstfruits, please rephrase James 1:18 in your own words.

    _____

    _____

Did you catch the fact that God **chose** *to give us spiritual birth through Jesus? Now, why would He willingly choose to do that? Colossians 1:19 says that God was also* **pleased** *to have all his fullness dwell in Him (Jesus).*

Let's read Colossians 1:15-23 together.

- What do you learn about Jesus in these verses?_____

    _____

- What do you learn about God in these verses? _____

    _____

- Why was God pleased in the shedding of Jesus' blood?_____

_____

- What are the benefits for us as believers in the sacrificial death of Jesus?

_____

How has God spoken to you in today's lesson? _____

_____

Lesson 3

James 1:19-27

We're going to be focusing on James 1:19-20 today. James immediately starts out with "take note of this." He wants us to sit up straight, eyes forward, get out a paper and pencil because what he has to say next is something important.

- Of what does James want us to take special note? *"Everyone should be quick to _____, slow to _____ and slow to _____."*

Do you think this may be the reason God gave us two ears and only one mouth! (Sigh.......if only we actually used our ears twice as much as our mouths.) ☺ Why is it that our tendency is to half listen to what someone is saying and then shoot off our mouth either in anger or with our opinion?

- What do the following verses say about anger:

  II Corinthians 12:20 _____

  Ephesians 4:_____

  Colossians 3:8 _____

  1 Timothy 2:8 _____

Now for the $50-million-dollar-question: Is anger wrong? Let's turn to Ephesians 4:26-27 for help with this question.

- What does the first part of vs. 26 say? _____

Anger is a feeling like any other. If you've ever attended a marriage conference or spent any time in marital counseling, you may remember the statement: "Feelings are neither right nor wrong." Feelings are just that-- feelings. It's what we do with those feelings that determine if sin is involved.

- What is the warning given in vs. 26 & 27? _____

  _____

- What do you think is meant by not letting the sun go down while you are still angry?

  _____

- How do you think this would be giving the devil a foothold? _____

  _____

Did you happen to notice in James 1:20 that he specified the anger he was referring to as "man's anger?" (Yes, ladies, that includes us as well.) The implication is that there is more than one kind of anger. Our anger is generally self-centered: I was rejected; I was used; I was misunderstood; I was hurt; I was treated unfairly. And we want to get even or get revenge.

- What does James say is the result of man's anger?_____

_____

The Greek word for "righteous" is described as equity (of character or act). So we could say that our human anger does not reflect a life that fairly and justly represents the character and nature of God. That being said, is there anger that would reflect God accurately?

Let's look at a couple of examples of anger in and from the life of Jesus.

- Please read Mark 2:23-3:6 and summarize the issue between Jesus and the Pharisees (religious leaders).

_____

_____

- What was the purpose of the Sabbath? (Exodus 20:8-11) _____

_____

- Why do you think Jesus was angry with the Pharisees?_____

_____

Jewish tradition had so increased the requirements and restrictions for keeping the Sabbath that it had become intolerable. The Pharisees believed that Jesus healing on the Sabbath constituted "work," and therefore broke the Jewish Sabbath law. Through His healing, Jesus challenged these man-made traditions and emphasized God's original purpose of the Sabbath--a day of spiritual, mental and physical restoration for man.

Please read another example of Jesus' anger in John 2:13-16.

- What is the Jewish Passover? (see Exodus 12:21-28)_____

_____

_____

Jews who travelled long distances in order to celebrate the Passover Feast in Jerusalem had to purchase an animal or dove for the required sacrifice. Coins first had to be exchanged by travelers into currency acceptable to the temple authorities before they could make their purchase. Both the moneychangers and the merchants selling the animals were necessary; however, rather than set up their businesses away from the temple, the merchants had set up booths in the outer courts of God's holy temple in order to conduct their transactions.

- Why do you think Jesus was so angry at these merchants? _____

  _____

- Read and summarize Isaiah 29:13 for additional insight into Jesus' anger.

  _____

  _____

God's anger is always right and just. His anger burns against those like the Pharisees and merchants who practice religion for show or profit while having absolutely no relationship with God. In their hypocrisy, they keep others from a pure and meaningful relationship with God through their rules and traditions.

- Can you give an example of anger you may have experienced that would reflect the heart of God accurately?

  _____

  _____

How has God spoken to you in today's lesson? _____

_____

We'll be focusing on James 1:21 today. Notice how he starts right out with the word "therefore." James uses this to connect what he previously said with what he is now about to say. We could translate verse 21 another way: because our anger does not accurately reflect who God is and how He wants us to represent Him, we need to get rid of (put aside) moral filth and evil and accept (put on) God's word with humility.

- As a quick review, list below some of the things that God sees as moral filth from 1 Peter 2:1 and Ephesians 4:31.

_____

Along with moral filth, James also cautions us to get rid of "the evil that is so prevalent" (widespread or superior). Do you remember why evil is so prevalent (review vs. 14)? It's those pesky evil desires that live within each one of us. James not only challenges us to get rid of something, but he then tells us to "put on" something else in its place--the Word.

The idea of removal and replacement is a theme consistent throughout the Bible. Jesus uses an illustration to make this point in **Luke 11:24-26.**

- What point do you believe Jesus was trying to make in this story? _____

_____

The picture Jesus uses of a house is symbolic of our heart. Evil was removed from the heart, and it was "swept clean and put in order." That's great! Sin was removed. Although it had been swept clean, it was left unoccupied. If we remove sin from our lives without replacing it with God's presence (His spirit and Word), we invite disaster.

- From the following verses, what are we to remove and with what are we to replace it?

	Put aside	Put on
Romans 13:12-14	_____	_____
Ephesians 4:22-24	_____	_____
Colossians 3:8-12	_____	_____

*It's easy to read about removing the old and putting on the new, but **how** do we go about doing that? What does it look like in everyday living?*

- From the following verses, comment on how you, personally, would "put on" the new self (thoughts, heart, actions).

  Romans 12:2 _____

  _____

  Philippians 4:8-9 _____

  _____

  Colossians 3:1-2 _____

  _____

Let's go back to James 1:21. After we remove moral filth and evil, James tells us to "humbly accept the word planted in you..." What exactly does it mean to humbly accept--for that matter, what does it mean to accept something? One of the definitions of "accept" is "to take or receive something offered." Another is "to regard as true or sound; believe."

- Can you think of some things that we might accept without believing?

  _____

The kind of acceptance that James is talking about has to do with an openness of the heart: to receive favorably, give ear to, embrace, make one's own.

- What do you think it would mean to "humbly accept" in the context of verse 21?

  _____

- Read Isaiah 45:18-24. Please share the verses that spoke to you personally causing you to feel humbled before your God?

  _____

- Read and summarize Isaiah 55:8-9. _____

  _____

Humility means that while we don't always understand everything about God, His ways or His word, we know HE IS GOD (and we are not). Because of this, we can fully accept His word as truth because of He who holds the truth in His hands.

How has God spoken to you in today's lesson? _____

_____

Please read James 1:22-24.

James transitions now from encouraging us to have an open-hearted accepting belief of the word planted in our hearts to a warning against being deceived. The bottom line is this: accepting God's word should bring about changes in our behavior and not just increased knowledge. The analogy he uses hits a bull's eye because as we all know, ladies, the mirror never lies! Isn't that unfortunate?

- What difference do you see between vs. 16 & 22? _____

    _____

Did you catch the difference? This is very similar to what we discovered about evil; it comes from without and also from our own evil desires within us. Likewise, not only can we be deceived, but we can also deceive ourselves.

- What do the following verses have to say about being deceived?

    Romans 7:7-11 _____

    Romans 16:17-18 _____

    2 Corinthians 11:3-4 _____

- Can you share an example of a time when you were deceived by sin?

    _____

    _____

In the context of the verses we're studying today regarding deception, James is warning us not to deceive ourselves (because it's so easy to do). Let's face it, if we work hard enough at it, we can justify and rationalize anything that we want to do regardless of what God's word has to say. For a real eye-opener, check out the below definitions.

- <u>Justify</u>: to defend or uphold as warranted or well-grounded.

- <u>Rationalize</u>: to credit one's acts, opinions, etc. to causes that superficially seem reasonable and valid but that actually are unrelated to the true.

Translation: If I'm not careful, I can wind up defending or upholding my actions, thoughts and/or opinions as reasonable, solid and valid even if they are not in line with the truth of God's word.

- What do the following verses have to say about deceiving ourselves?

Obadiah 3 _____

1 Corinthians 3:18-19 _____

1 John 1:8 _____

How do you view yourself? Have you ever heard the following statement: we see ourselves one way, others view us still another way, and the truth is somewhere in the middle? Do you see yourself as you want to be rather than how you really are?

- Why do you think most people struggle with having their picture taken or looking in a mirror?

_____

_____

James 1:22: "Do not merely listen to the word, and so deceive yourselves. Do what it says."

- Read vs. 23 again in context with vs. 22. What point do you think James was trying to make by using the analogy of our face and a mirror?

_____

_____

- John shares a hard truth in 1 John 2:3-4. Please read and summarize these verses.

_____

_____

A liar is a deceiver--whether it's lying to another person or to yourself. Are you being deceived (misled) into thinking that going to church or Bible study makes you a Christian by osmosis? Have you ever met someone who goes to every single Bible study year after year, never misses a week, and yet never seems to change or grow in relationship with God? Why is that?

Fill in the below from John 14:21:

Whoever has my _____ and _____ them, he is the

_____ _____ _____ _____.

Personal. Look truthfully in the mirror. Has the Holy Spirit been speaking to you about a particular area of disobedience in your life that you may be rationalizing because you like it, don't want to give it up or are, perhaps, afraid of the consequences? Obedience is how we show our love to God. There is a promise in 1 John 1:8-9 that we need to remember. While we deceive ourselves if we claim to be without sin, God also promises that, "If we confess our sins, he is faithful and just and will forgive us our sins and purify us from all unrighteousness."

How has God spoken to you in today's lesson? _____

_____

What does the word "budget" bring to your mind? Do you get a sense of confinement or freedom? How about laws and rules? In our human nature, we see these things as restrictive--a set of "dos" and "don'ts" just made to control us and take away our fun. Since we're focusing on James 1:25 today, we'll need to try and understand what on earth James means when he talks about "the perfect law that gives freedom." Isn't that a bit of an oxymoron? How can law bring freedom? What law is he talking about?

In the most general sense, when God's word talks about "the law," it is referring to the 10 Commandments that God gave to Moses to govern and guide the children of Israel. (Deuteronomy 5:6-21). Below is a summary of the commandments:

THE TEN COMMANDMENTS
1. Do not worship other gods.
2. Do not worship idols.
3. Do not misuse God's name.
4. Keep the Sabbath holy.
5. Honor your father and mother.
6. Do not murder.
7. Do not commit adultery.
8. Do not steal.
9. Do not lie.
10. Do not covet.

- On the above, put a "G" by the commandments that focus on our relationship with God and an "O" by those that focus on our relationship with others.

- What did Jesus have to say about the commandments according to Matthew 22:36-40?

_____

_____

For simplicity of today's study, when God's word refers to "the law," the inference is anything referring to our relationship with God and/or our relationship with others as opposed to the Levitical Law which focuses on physical requirements in order to meet God's standard of holiness.

Let's read together Galatians 3:15-25

- What was the purpose of the law? _____

What on earth does Paul mean when he says that the law was added because of transgressions (sin)? Think about it this way. If you're driving down a road with no traffic signs, you can drive at whatever speed you want. The minute a sign is posted stating that the speed limit is 45 mph and you go above that speed limit, you are breaking the law, correct? You are now aware that a) there is a law, and b) you have broken the law.

- What do you think Paul meant in vs. 24 when he said that the law was put in charge to lead us to Christ?

_____

_____

How can we understand that we are sinners and in need of a Savior unless we are aware of God's requirements (commandments) for life and our awareness that we cannot possibly live each and every day in line with those requirements? When we "miss the mark" in living up to God's standards, it is called SIN. The wonderful news is that we have not been left hopeless in our sin.

- What hope are we given in Romans 8:1-4? _____

_____

We've partially answered the question of how the law can bring freedom, haven't we? We receive freedom from sin through the death of Jesus on the cross. AMEN and HALLELUJAH! But, the good news is that we receive other benefits of freedom as well as forgiveness of sins. Look at a couple of definitions of "freedom" below:

1) Ease or facility of movement or action
2) The right to enjoy all the privileges or special rights of citizenship.

*Look at the second definition. Jesus' purchase of our freedom from sin gives us the right to enjoy **all** God's privileges and rights because we are members of the Kingdom of God. God's promises are for us, His children!*

- Do you struggle with believing God's promises are for you? If so, why?

_____

Regarding the first definition of freedom, rules and regulations (laws) help us determine what our boundaries are, don't they? Boundaries give us a sense of security because we know the rules of the game, so to speak. When we live within God's boundaries, we have ease (peace of mind) in our actions and movements; we know we are pleasing God.

- What promise are we given in James 1:25 if we live according to God's laws?

_____

Another word for "blessed" is "happy." If we live under God's law, we will be happy in what we do. Years ago, there was a little children's book called, "Doing Right Makes Me Happy." Does it get any simpler than that? God has designed us to be truly happy and fulfilled when we are living under his commands. Our little children's book could be titled, "Pleasing God Makes Me Happy."

- What are the stipulations for enjoying this freedom and happiness?

  _____

- What does it mean to "look intently" into God's law (see also Psalm 1:1-2)?

  _____

- Read Psalm 19:7-10 to help answer the following:

  <u>God's law is:</u>   <u>God's law brings:</u>

  (ex.)   Perfect   Revival to the soul

  _____   _____

  _____   _____

  _____   _____

  _____   _____

  _____   _____

  _____   _____

  _____   _____

- Psalm 19:11: By them is your servant _____; in keeping them there is

  _____ .

We are told in James that we must regularly meditate intently (with purpose) on God's word and DO what it says to receive true freedom and fulfillment (blessings). Remember the old Nike ad? JUST DO IT. So, why don't we "just do it?"

- What hindrances and excuses keep you from "just doing it?" _____

  _____

How has God spoken to you in today's lesson? _____

_____

Today we finish up James chapter 1, focusing on vs. 26 & 27. This is another reminder about self-deception, the tongue, and keeping ourselves from moral pollution. Verse 22 told us that if we merely listen to the word and don't do what it says, we are deceiving ourselves; verse 26 tells us that if we can't control our tongues, we are also deceiving ourselves and our religion is worthless. Verse 19 taught us to be quick to listen, slow to speak and slow to become angry--another reminder on controlling our tongue. Finally, vs. 21 states that we need to get rid of all moral filth and evil, and vs. 27 follows up with a warning to keep ourselves from being polluted by the world.

Please reread James 1:19-25 adding also vs. 26 & 27.

The word translated "religious" in the Greek has to do with religious ritual but can also imply the internal piety of the worshiper. James uses both of these terms to speak of the right attitude of our heart in service to God but also spills over into a transformed life through our actions with others.

The idea of considering ourselves to be religious might be better translated in this context as anyone who seems to be religious or has the reputation of being religious. Either way, James is saying that if we can't control our tongue, our religion is worthless, and we are deceiving ourselves. James is going to delve deeper into the control of the tongue in chapter 3, so let's just focus on one aspect of the tongue in today's study--gossip.

-   What is **your** definition of the word "gossip?" _____

    _____

Very simply, a gossip is someone who idly talks about another person with regards to their personal or private life. There is probably not a woman alive who is not guilty of gossip at one time or another! An honest look at the heart's motive is the determining factor in our action.

-   What are some ways we could perhaps deceive ourselves regarding gossip?

    _____

    _____

-   What do the following verses say about gossip?

    Proverbs 11:13 _____

    Proverbs 16:28 _____

    Proverbs 18:8 _____

- Why do you think our religion would be considered worthless if our tongue is out of control?

  _____

  _____

- What does God consider to be true religion? (James 1:27) _____

  _____

The theme continues--our relationship with God and our relationship with others. Taking care of the needs of orphans and widows in their distress is one example of our relationship with others through action; keeping ourselves from being polluted by the immorality of the world has everything to do with keeping an open and honest relationship with God.

One of the synonyms for pollution is "contamination" which means "making impure or unsuitable by contact or mixture with something unclean, bad, etc..."

Read 1 John 2:15-17

- What are we warned of in vs. 15? _____

- What things come from the world? (vs. 16) _____

- Why are we not to love the world? (vs. 17) _____

- Read Colossians 2:20 and list some of the things you believe to be the "basic principles of this world." _____

  _____

  _____

- According to Romans 12:2, what is the secret to staying uncontaminated by the world?

  _____

- What do you think it means to be "transformed by the renewing of your mind?"

  _____

How has God spoken to you in today's lesson? _____

_____

Lesson 4

James 2:1-13

James chapter 1 is considered the introduction to the book of James with chapters 2-5 regarded as the main body of the letter. After the greeting in James 1:1, James then starts into the first of his two-part introduction. Verse 12, used more as a parenthetical verse, does not really belong to either part of the introduction but serves more as a transitional verse. The breakdown below shows the correlation of the topics covered in each part of the introduction.

Introduction Part 1	Introduction Part 2
James 1:2-11	**James 1:13-27**
Spiritual Benefit of Trials	Self-deception Regarding Temptation
Godly Wisdom	Self-deception Regarding Godly Living
Wise Attitudes for Rich & Poor	Self-deception Regarding Religious Practice

James immediately starts out in the main part of the letter (chapter 2) addressing the issue of favoritism. He is focusing in part on the law from Leviticus 19:15 which says:

Do not pervert justice; do not show _____ to the _____ or

_____ to the _____, but judge your neighbor fairly.

James' main focus is the apparent problem of favoritism towards the rich in the Christian community and uses a supposed hypothetical example (which was probably a real life situation) to make his point.

- Read James 2:1-4 and summarize the problem and the example James gives:

_____

_____

Is favoritism the same as prejudice? You be the judge. See the definitions below:

    Favoritism – favoring of one person or group over others with equal claims; discrimination.

    Prejudice – Preconceived opinion or feeling, either favorable or unfavorable.

- Based on these definitions, do you see these as similar or different?

_____

_____

Either way, James is addressing a specific problem--the attitude of the heart. God is not prejudice, does not show favoritism or discriminate, and neither should we as believers.

Please read 1 Samuel 16:1-13

At God's request, Samuel was asked to anoint a new king for Israel of God's choosing. Samuel was blind to everything but the fact that it was one of the sons of Jesse.

- On what basis was Samuel apparently judging who should be king? _____

- Did Samuel show prejudice in this situation? If so, how? _____
  _____

- What was God's response to Samuel in vs. 7? _____
  _____

- The second part of verse 7 says, "*the Lord looks at the heart.*" (vs. 7b) Does that statement bring you comfort or discomfort? Why?
  _____

- Why do you think we are so quick to form judgments based on outward appearances?
  _____
  _____

How about you? Are you quick to form opinions of others based on external first impressions? Do you tend to spend time with those who are "like you?" Does your ministry to and investment in others lean towards those who most look, act and think like you? When you see new visitors at church, do you gravitate towards those you consider to be most appropriately dressed and groomed?

These are hard questions to have to consider, and it would be very easy to just check off the list and say "no" to all. Honestly and humbly ask God to show you if and where you struggle with prejudice, and allow Him time and opportunity to respond to you. While God's truth may be uncomfortable at first, we cannot open the door of our heart for the Holy Spirit to work change <u>until</u> we are open and honest before God.

How has God spoken to you in today's lesson? _____
_____

The Christian community in James' day bears a striking similarity to the present, doesn't it? Favoritism, discrimination and prejudice are just as evident in the Christian community today as they were two thousand years ago whether we want to admit it or not. What is it about human nature that wants to sum up a person after one glance as either worthy or unworthy, stable or unstable, rich or poor, needy or emotionally healthy? What is it about a person that appears "together" in dress, manner and attitude that lends to a quicker acceptance and/or tolerance of their personal character defects (which God likes to call "sin").

James addressed a hypothetical church situation regarding the apparent favoritism of a rich person by giving special attention and the best seat while basically telling the poor person to just stand in the back or sit on the floor.

Then in today's verses, James asks his readers a redundant question: "Isn't it the rich who are exploiting you? Aren't they the ones who are dragging you into court? Aren't they the ones who are slandering the noble name of Him to whom you belong?" Clearly, the "rich" to whom he's referring here aren't believers or they wouldn't be slandering the name of Jesus. However, he is clearly making a point. You think the rich are better and so favor them, and yet look at how the rich are treating you.

Read James 2:5-7 along with Galatians 3:26-29.

- According to Galatians, how are we all considered equal or "as one?"

_____

Based on God's values, the poor, who are defined by how little they own, are destined to inherit God's kingdom. The focus here is not on poverty; rather, James is saying that a poor person, as part of the Christian community, shares the privileges and status of God's kingdom. This is what makes favoritism in the church so appalling; it is in direct conflict to God's values .

Let's talk about this kingdom we are to inherit. Jesus has much to say about this. What is Jesus trying to convey about *entering* the Kingdom of Heaven from the below verses?

- Matthew 7:21 _____

_____

- Matthew 18:1-4 _____

_____

While the above verses focus on *entering* the kingdom of heaven, the below focus on what the kingdom of heaven is like. Please summarize.

- Matthew 13:31-32 _____

  _____

- Matthew 13:44&45 _____

- Matthew 18:21-35 _____

- Matthew 20:1-16 _____

  _____

- Luke 17:20-21 _____

- Based on the above, how would you summarize the kingdom of heaven?

  _____

  _____

Did you catch it? The kingdom of heaven lives in us as believers teaching us to surrender all to God, to forgive others, not to look at "fairness" from our perspective and to know that the kingdom grows within us in order to benefit others.

- According to James 2:5 and Galatians 3:29, how are we made heirs to this kingdom?

  _____

- What guarantee has God given us of our inheritance? (See Ephesians 1:13-14)

  _____

Think about this for a minute. The kingdom of heaven lives in us in the form of the Holy Spirit giving us a guarantee that we will truly inherit the kingdom of God (eternal life). Now how's that for air-tight assurance from God?

How has God spoken to you in today's lesson? _____

_____

Yesterday, we talked about the kingdom that we will one day inherit and which also lives within us. Where there is a kingdom, there is a King, and as with any king, royalty follows. Royalty is the status, dominion, authority or power of a sovereign; a sovereign, then, is the one who has supreme rank, power or authority. When we live within the kingdom of God, Jesus Christ is our King, our Sovereign. Amen!

Our verse today in James 2:8 talks about the royal law. Please read vs. 8. It's called the "royal law" because it is the supreme law that is the source of all other laws governing human relationships. It is the foundation for how people treat each other in the kingdom of God under the rule of the king.

- What exactly is the royal law?_____

In Deuteronomy chapter 5, God clearly laid out his Ten Commandments which focus on loving Him and loving others; however, knowing our human nature and how we look for ways around the law, he spelled things out in an even more detailed way by providing various additional laws so we would clearly understand his heart's intent for the way we are to live in His kingdom.

- Read Leviticus 19:11-18. How is the second part of verse 18 a summary of all the other verses?

  _____

- According to Matthew 22:34-40, what was the standard Jesus gave for how we were to love others?

  _____

We are told to love our neighbor as ourselves, and yet in Philippians 2:3-4, it says, "Do nothing out of selfish ambition or vain conceit, but in humility consider others better than yourselves." How do I love me while at the same time consider others better than myself? Not only that, I'm not all that sure that I even love myself.

- What does Ephesians 5:29 say? _____

Do you care for and feed your body? If you're reading this, then the answer to that has to be "yes," doesn't it? Now, you may not like particular physical aspects or personality traits about yourself, but that is entirely different than loving yourself.

- Please explain how we are to love ourselves and at the same time to think of others as better than ourselves. See also Philippians 2:4.

  _____

It's all about balance. How can we care for others if we aren't caring for ourselves? Caring for ourselves involves much more than just taking care of our basic needs. It's not just about eating, but eating balanced and healthy; it's not just getting enough sleep, but also getting rest. Rest is so much more than just sleeping; it's a period of **calm** *inactivity after labor or exertion.*

Does the concept of inactivity seem foreign to you? Do you feel guilty if you relax? Do you feel like you're always running but never getting anywhere? Does inactivity seem unproductive to you?

-   Genesis 2:2 says, "By the seventh day God had finished the work he had been doing; so on the seventh day he _____ "

-   Was God really tired from spending energy on creating the universe? What does Isaiah 40:28 say? _____

-   If God never tires, why do you think he chose to rest from all his labor on the seventh day? _____

Do you think God was trying to tell us something by His example of resting? Let's not confuse inactivity with laziness. A lazy person is someone who doesn't like to work or exert themselves in any way; that's not at all what we are talking about here.

I'm sure we can all understand the concept of inactivity, but what about the **calm** *part -- relief from troubles or burdens; freedom from worry, agitation or excitement; tranquility. Does this seem unattainable to you because you tend to sit and stew? Worry and wait?*

If we don't know how to rest (attain calm inactivity), how can we have a balanced spiritual life in relationship with God?

Let's take a quick detour to the home of Mary and Martha. **Please read Luke 10:38-42.**

-   What was Martha's complaint, and how did Jesus respond to her?

    _____

    _____

Read Matthew 11:28-30

-   What three things does Jesus ask us to do? _____

-   What promise does Jesus give us?_____

Jesus tells us to come to him, take his yoke and learn from him, and we will find rest for our souls. Doesn't that feel like a breath of fresh air? What does he want us to learn from him?

Summarize the following verses:

- Mark 1:35 _____

- Mark 6:31 _____

- Luke 5:15-16 _____

- John 8:28-29 _____

He wants us to learn balance--to pull away and spend alone time with Him, to pull away and rest, to pray, and to do what pleases God.

Go back to Luke 10:38-42 for a moment. Jesus told Martha that Mary sitting at His feet was the "only thing <u>needed</u>," and that Mary had chosen "what was better." It's not about the "doing," it's about the "being." Jesus knows we <u>need</u> spiritual feeding; the activities and routine of life will come out of our relationship with Him; our need is for the kingdom of God to reign over our natural human mindset and behavior.

Balance is sitting at the feet of Jesus and spending time with Him.

- So how are you doing in this area?

_____

_____

Tomorrow we will turn our focus to the first part of the royal law--loving our neighbor.

How has God spoken to you in today's lesson? _____

_____

Let's read today's verses. The ongoing theme of self-deception is implied in verses 9-11. Verse 10 states that "whoever keeps the whole law and yet stumbles at just one point is guilty of breaking all of it." Basically, James is saying, "Don't be fooled. Even though you may not have committed adultery or murder, if you've lied to or cheated someone, you're still a lawbreaker." The law is the expression of the character and will of God; therefore, to violate one part of the law is to violate God's will and consequently His whole law.

The royal law speaks of loving our neighbor as ourselves. Yesterday, we talked about the "loving ourselves" part of this law; today we will focus on what "loving our neighbor" looks like. There are a few questions we will have to answer in order to get a clearer picture of this command: 1) Who is my neighbor? 2) What does God's love look like? 3) What does loving my neighbor really mean? 4) How can I live out God's love?

1. **Who is my neighbor?**

   Read Luke 10:25-37 and summarize the parable Jesus told in answer to this question.

   _____

   _____

Now, it's clear that a neighbor can be anyone, not just those living close to us. It certainly broadens the commandment to "love our neighbor," doesn't it?

2. **What does God's love look like?**

   What do the following verses have to say about God's love?

   1 John 4:9-10 _____

   Romans 5:8 _____

1 Corinthians 13:4-7 clearly defines what God's love looks like. List the attributes you have found.

_____

_____

_____

_____

3. **What does loving my neighbor really mean?**

We've been shown quite extensively in 1 Corinthians 13 the attributes of love as seen from the eyes of God. One of these attributes, "Love keeps no record of wrongs," plays a huge part in what loving our neighbor really means. We can only be in relationship with God because of His forgiveness of our sins through the death of His Son, Jesus; we cannot be in close relationship with others or God unless we can offer this same kind of forgiveness.

- Please read Matthew 6:9-15. What specifically does verse 12 say?

_____

Jesus was teaching His followers how to pray. In asking God to forgive us of our debts (sin, trespass, something owed) the implication is that we have <u>already forgiven</u> those who have wronged or sinned against us <u>before</u> we've come asking God's forgiveness.

- What is the stipulation Jesus gave in receiving forgiveness from God?

_____

Ouch! Does it really say that? Not only does it, but they are the very words of Jesus Christ Himself. To put the concept of forgiveness into perspective, Jesus tells a story to illustrate this point.

- Please read Matthew 18:21-35. What was Jesus' perspective on forgiveness in this story?_____

_____

A man owed his master $16 million dollars; the man did not have the money to pay him so the master cancelled the man's debt completely. The forgiven man then turned around and went to someone who owed him $25 and told him basically to "pay up or go to jail." Since the man couldn't pay the debt, he was thrown in jail.

We read this and think how unfair the first man was to the poor man who only owed him $25, because we understand the story from God's perspective as Jesus intended. However, when we fail to forgive someone for an injustice done to us, we've lost perspective. We devalue our sin towards God as only worth $25, and we increase the value of another's sin toward us ($16 million).

- Why is forgiving others so difficult?_____

_____

When we are confronted with having to forgive another person (no matter how horrible the injustice done to us), two statements immediately surface: "It's not fair!" and "If I forgive them, then I'm condoning what they've done to me." Please understand this: <u>Life is not always fair. Period! It just isn't!</u> The sooner you accept this fact (whether you want it to be so or not), the quicker you can move into forgiveness. "Acid corrodes the container." This just means that bitterness and unforgiveness will eat you alive.

The deception in the second statement that we are somehow condoning a person's wrong action if we forgive them is just that—deception. It is a lie from the pit of hell! If you lie to someone knowing that Colossians 3:9 says: "Do not lie to each other," and then you come asking God's forgiveness for the lie, does His forgiveness mean that He condones the fact that you lied and, therefore, negates His word? Absolutely not! He simply understands that you are aware of your sin in contrast to His standard, have come to Him in repentance asking for forgiveness, and He has graciously chosen to forgive you. But it NEVER changes God's standard - ever!

- Personal. Are you holding bitterness and unforgiveness in your heart? Have you somehow allowed Satan to skew your perspective on what you believe you are owed as opposed to how God has forgiven you?

1. **How can I live out God's love?**

   - Read Colossians 3:12-14 and list the actions we are to take?

   _____

First and foremost in living out God's love is making the mental choice to do so. The idea of "clothing ourselves" and "putting on" are choices that require action on our part. Making the mental determination to love according to God's standard lays the groundwork for God to "do his thing."

   - According to 2 Corinthians 12:9-10, how do you think we can become strong through our weaknesses?

   _____

We must humbly come before God admitting that we cannot love on our own. Our nature is weak and wants its own way. We want to get even; we want revenge; we just plain don't want to forgive.

The good news is that we haven't been left to figure out how to love others based simply on our own weak, human efforts. We have a promise!

Read 2 Peter 1:3-4. These are powerful words!

- According to vs. 3, what have we been given and why?

_____

- What are God's promises based on? _____

- What do God's promises allow us to participate in and escape from?

_____

We cannot take His power lightly. He has made it available to us, His children. Listen to what Ephesians 1:19-20 has to say: "... and his **incomparably great power** for us who believe. That **power** is like the working of His mighty strength which He exerted in Christ when He raised him from the dead and seated Him at His right hand in the heavenly realms..."

Did you catch it? We have access to the power of God--the same power that He used to raise Jesus Christ from the dead. It's for us, His believers, to help us in living and loving according to His standards.

- Ask yourself honestly if you believe this to be true FOR YOU!

How has God spoken to you in today's lesson? _____

_____

There's an uncomfortable similarity in today's verses that ring from yesterday regarding the idea of reaping what we sow. The forgiveness we have towards others is in direct relation to the forgiveness God will show us. In today's lesson, the same standard of measurement is set, but this time it's pertaining to mercy and judgment. If you give no mercy, you will receive judgment without mercy. In a sense, though, it's really just another name for judging in unforgiveness because mercy is the discretionary power of a judge to pardon someone or to lessen punishment.

James is effectively turning the tables by first showing that when we show favoritism to the rich and discriminate against the poor, we have become "judges with evil thoughts" (vs 4). Now he is saying that if we continue to judge without mercy, a time will come when we, too, will stand before God on the side of being judged without mercy.

- Take a moment to read today's verses from James along with Matthew 7:1-5 and then summarize verses 1 & 2 in the Matthew passage.

  _____

- How does Jesus again illustrate the idea of perspective in relation to judgment from verses 3-5 in Matthew?

  _____

  _____

Our sin is the plank that we neglect while we are busy judging another for the speck of sin in their eye. It's so much easier to focus on someone else's shortcomings and faults rather than look at our own, isn't it? Jesus is again reminding us to stop looking outward and start looking inward. Keep perspective. We are being hypocritical if we think we can see clearly past our own sin in order to judge another person.

Jesus tells us to be careful in judging because the measure we use will be used to judge us. This judgment isn't for determining our eternal destiny, but more likely with regards to our eternal rewards.

Please read 1 Corinthians 3:11-15.

- What do you think Paul means by building with gold, silver and costly stones?

  _____

- What do you think is meant by building with wood, hay or straw?

  _____

How can we be assured that what we are building for eternity will not go up in flames on the "day of judgment?" That's easy. Ephesians 5:10 says to "find out what pleases the Lord." So how do we do that?

Are you aware that right now you are finding out what pleases God? That's right, going to Bible study is one way to do just that along with going to church, spending time with other Christians, prayer and your own personal alone time with God in His word. All of these (and many more) will help you in knowing what pleases God.

The foundation for pleasing God comes from one thing only according to Hebrews 11:6.

- What is the foundation? _____

- Why is it so important? _____

- What are we promised? _____

Let's go back to 1 Corinthians 3:11-15 looking again with the understanding that without faith we cannot please God.

- Have you received any additional insight into the idea of building with gold, silver, costly stones or wood, hay or straw?

  _____

- What exactly does verse 11 say? For no one can lay any _____

  other than the one already laid, which is _____ _____ .

Faith is our foundation--faith in God the Father and Jesus Christ, His Son. What we do in service for God will either be done in faith for His glory (gold, silver, costly stones) or done for our own self-glorification (wood, hay, straw). How do we know the difference? Ask yourself who's receiving the glory, God or you? Is your work something God has asked from you or something you think you "should" do as a Christian? Perhaps, you feel that there isn't anyone else qualified or capable to handle the task. Maybe you just like the feeling of importance and attention you get when performing this particular task or ministry.

- How are you currently serving God in faith, or are you serving at all? How have you personally received assurance that what you're doing pleases him by your faith? Please share.

  _____

  _____

*2 Corinthians 5:9-10 says, "So we **make it our goal to please him**, whether we are at home in the body or away from it. For we must all appear before the judgment seat of Christ, that each one may receive what is due him for the things done while in the body, whether good or bad."*

Do you become fearful in thinking about the "day of judgment?" Let God's word remove any fear you may have.

Please read 1 John 4:13-18.

- In what do we have confidence on the day of judgment?

  _____

- What drives out fear from punishment? _____

Verse 16 states, "And so we know and rely on the love God has for us. God is love. Whoever lives in love lives in God, and God in Him." Amen! That's our hope and confidence. Because God is love, we can with assurance rely on His love for us. Wonderful, isn't it?!!

How has God spoken to you in today's lesson? _____

_____

Notes

Lesson 5

James 2:14-26

What is true faith and what does it look like? Trust (a synonym for faith) is defined as "reliance on the integrity, strength, ability, etc... of a person or thing; confidence." Let's look at the following story to try and help us understand and perhaps answer the question regarding true faith.

Niagara Falls lies on the border of Ontario, Canada, and New York State with the highest part of the Falls at 180 feet. The first of many tightrope walkers to cross the Falls was Jean Francois Gravelot, a French aerialist, who called himself "The Great Blondin" because of his fair hair. Born February 28, 1824, Blondin had been walking the tightrope since the age of five. In 1851, at the age of twenty-seven, he joined the Ravel troupe of French equestrian and acrobatic performers on their tour of North America.

On June 30, 1859, Blondin made his first journey across the Falls. For two summers, Blondin performed above the Niagara. During his many performances, he crossed the Falls on a bicycle, on stilts, and at night. He swung by one arm, turned somersaults, and stood on his head on a chair. Once he pushed a stove in a wheelbarrow and cooked an omelet; another time he crossed blindfolded in a heavy sack made of blankets. People came from all over to watch him perform believing him capable of performing each and every stunt he said he could do.

Now, imagine him looking straight at you and asking, "Do you believe I can walk across the Falls blindfolded?"

You reply, "Yes, I do."

He then asks you, "Do you believe I can carry someone across on my back while blindfolded?"

"Of course, you reply."

"Will you get on my back then?" he asks you.

Silence follows.........

Was your belief in Blondin's capabilities true and sincere? Did you have confidence in and reliance on his integrity, strength and abilities? If so, then <u>*why didn't you get on his back*</u>*???? James stated, "...faith by itself, if it is not accompanied by action, is dead."*

Please read James 2:14-17.

I'm sure we've all heard someone say at one time or another that their faith is "private" and not something they talk about. Is "private" faith really faith at all? Self-deception has been central in James' writings so far. He states we are deceiving ourselves if we listen without doing, if we cannot control our tongue, or if we say we have faith but there is no accompanying action.

The question, then, that must be asked is, "How is true faith evidenced?"

Please read Colossians 1:10-12. According to verse 10, how and what are we to produce (bear)?

_____

Please read and summarize Matthew 7:15-18. _____

_____

_____

From Galatians 5:22-23, please list some of the "fruit" that Jesus is talking about.

_____

Colossians 3:12-14 lists some additional virtues with which we are to clothe ourselves (bear).

How does verse 14 summarize the virtues? _____

_____

*Every Christian virtue comes from love. Love is not just one of the characteristics; love **is** the fruit, and it's evidenced by gentleness, kindness, patience, forgiveness, etc.*

From 1 John 3:16-20, please answer the following:

- How do we know what love is? _____

- What evidence would be shown if the love of God were truly in us?

   _____

- How do we know we belong to the truth and have peace in God's presence?

   _____

Did you happen to notice in Galatians 5 that the characteristics of Christian fruit are referred to as the fruit of the Spirit? Jesus taught his followers on this very thing. Let's turn to John 15:1-5.

- What is needed in order for us to bear fruit? _____

- What do you think Jesus meant when he said, "Apart from me, you can do nothing?"

   _____

   _____

Please turn to and read John 14:15-18.

- What was Jesus' promise to his followers in vs. 18? _____

- How would Jesus come to us? _____

Galatians 5:25 says "Since we live by the Spirit, let us keep in step with the Spirit." The Spirit is Jesus; Jesus is the Spirit. Keeping in step with the Spirit means walking and living with Jesus and like Jesus. Without the Spirit we cannot bear eternal fruit; we can do nothing of eternal value.

How has God spoken to you in today's lesson? _____

_____

James continues his dialogue from verses 16 and 17 regarding faith and action; a believer is in need of food and clothes and is told by another believer that he will pray for him. James responds, "How does that help his physical needs?" "Faith is not real and alive if there is no corresponding action." The person retorts, "You have faith; I have deeds."

James then goes on to state that it isn't an either/or situation--faith or deeds. How can true faith be evidenced without deeds (action)? Go on, try and show me your faith apart from action; I'll show you my faith by my action. Do you really think that just believing in God is all it takes? Why even the demons believe in God! Does that belief make them followers of God? Absolutely not! James then goes on in the rest of chapter two to give supporting evidence as to why true faith can only be evidenced by action.

Confusion often springs up when we look at verses like John 3:16 and Romans 3:22-24? What do these verses say?

John 3:16 _____

Romans 3:22-24 _____

_____

These verses say that we're saved by grace through faith in Jesus Christ, period! They absolutely do; however, we cannot take these verses and isolate them from the rest of God's word in order to make a "faith only" case. Perhaps, the below verses will help clear things up a bit.

Let's read Ephesians 2:8-10 together.

- What does verse 8 say? _____

- According to verse 9, why can't our works save us?

_____

*Clear as mud now, right? Is God contradicting himself? Never! Faith in Jesus is the **only** way we can be made right with God. Nothing we ever do can aid in our salvation--it's a gift from God. We can never take credit for our salvation. However, what makes our faith a true, saving faith?*

- Read and summarize verse 10. _____

_____

We aren't saved by works or from works, but <u>we are saved for works.</u>

Hebrews chapter 11 is appropriately titled "The Hall of Faith." Please take a minute to read this chapter slowly and prayerfully.

-   List an example from this chapter regarding faith in action.

    _____

    _____

Did you happen to catch the first part of verse 39? "These were all commended

_____   _____   _____ ..."

Let's focus on the practical, active faith of Noah for a moment by re-reading verse 7 of Hebrews along with Genesis 6:9-22?

-   What was the condition of the people of Noah's day? _____

    What do you learn about Noah in Genesis 6:9, 7:5 & 16?

    _____

-   According to Hebrews 11:7, what caused Noah to build the ark? _____

Noah's faith in the absolute certainty that God says what he means and means what he says caused him to build the ark. We are told that he was warned about "things not yet seen" in verse 7. In order to fully realize how dramatic Noah's faith truly was, we need to understand a couple of things about Noah and his circumstances.

Noah had never seen a flood; not only that, there is speculation as to whether Noah had ever even seen rain. Genesis 2:4-6 says:

> *"When the Lord God made the earth and the heavens - and no shrub of the field had yet appeared on the earth and no plant of the field had yet sprung up, for the Lord God had not sent rain on the earth and there was no man to work the ground, but streams came up from the earth and watered the whole surface of the ground...."*

Even if Noah had seen rain, he lived in a dry, landlocked region where it would be absolutely inconceivable that there would ever be enough water to float a vessel that was 450 feet tall x 75 feet wide x 45 feet tall.

Additionally, Noah was 500 yrs old when he became a father (Genesis 5:32), and the flood came when he was 600 yrs old (Genesis 7:11). Traditional belief is that it took Noah 120 years to build the ark. Genesis 6:3 alludes to this 120 years and 1 Peter 3:20 says, "... when God waited patiently in the days of Noah while the ark was being built."

Can you imagine the picture Noah must have made? Here he is building this BIG boat out in his driveway. When people would come by and ask him about it, he would go off on how a flood was coming to destroy everyone that didn't repent and turn back to God. Year after year after year people would walk by Noah's house laughing at him and yelling out taunts, "How's the boat coming, Noah? Where's all the water, huh? Shall I get my scuba gear ready?" And yet, Noah kept on building. Now that is faith in action!

Hebrews 11:6 tells us that "Without faith it is impossible to please God....." True faith is evidenced in our obedient action to God's word. There is no other way to prove our faith but to show it.

How has God spoken to you in today's lesson? _____

_____

In keeping with the idea of faith in action, James uses one of the premier examples of what this looks like in the life of Abraham. We will spend the next two days focusing on Abraham and his faith-full life. Abraham is known as the "Father of Righteousness" through faith.

If we remember that faith is being "sure of what we hope for and certain of what we do not see" (Hebrews 11:1), and righteousness is being made right with God, then "righteousness through faith" simply means that when I believe with absolute certainty in the existence and promises of God even though I cannot see any evidence, God considers me "right" or clean before him. The result is that I can now enter into a relationship with God. We'll talk more about this tomorrow.

Let's read our verses for today in James 2:20-22.

Confusion can easily come when we look at what James says in verse 21. "Was not our ancestor Abraham considered righteous for what he did when he offered his son Isaac on the altar?" So was he considered righteous by what he did or what he believed? Well, let's take a look back in Genesis.

- From Genesis 12:1-5, list the seven parts of the promise God makes to Abraham.

1. _____ 2. _____

3. _____ 4. _____

5. _____ 6. _____

7. _____

- How old was Abraham when God gave him this promise?_____

Read Genesis 15:1-5, 18 to help answer the following.

- What was Abraham's concern? _____

_____

- What promise did God give Abraham?_____

_____

- According to the following verses, who are Abraham's descendants?

  Acts 3:12,25 _____

  Galatians 3:8-9 _____

Let's turn to Genesis 21:1-7 to see the promise fulfilled.

- How old was Abraham when Isaac was born? _____

- How long did Abraham wait between the promise and the fulfillment? _____

Now that we understand the importance of the role Isaac was to have in regards to God's promise to Abraham, let's focus the rest of our time on Abraham's faith-filled actions.

Please read Genesis 22:1-14

- How did Abraham respond to God's command? _____

- What did Abraham believe? (vs. 5) _____

- Why do you think Isaac didn't struggle when Abraham bound him and placed him on the altar?

  _____

- Why did God test Abraham in this way? (vs. 12) _____

  _____

God used many events in the Old Testament to foreshadow future events that would be fulfilled by the coming of Jesus the Messiah. Does the story of Abraham and Isaac remind you of another story of love, obedience and sacrifice?

Let's look at a few of the similarities between this event in Genesis which God used to not only test Abraham's faith and obedience, but that he also used to foretell an event about His only Son, Jesus.

Please re-read and summarize the events in Genesis 22 focusing on the below verses on the left and how they were ultimately fulfilled by Jesus Christ.

Event in Genesis	Fulfillment by Jesus
vs. 2	John 3:16
vs. 6	John 19:16-17
vs. 8	John 1:29
vs. 13	1 John 2:2

Isn't it awesome how God spans time by foreshadowing an event that won't be fulfilled until thousands of years later? Isn't it comforting to know that God is awake and in control of the universe in which we live down to the most minute detail?

Let's close by reading Hebrews 11:17-19.

- Abraham's obedience to God's command to sacrifice his son Isaac was based on what belief?

_____

Wow! Abraham believed that God could raise the dead without ever having seen him do it. Now that's faith! Can you see a picture of yourself here? We were never an eyewitness to the actual resurrection of Jesus Christ from death, however, in faith we believe that God can do and did that very thing. Can you now see why we are considered Abraham's descendants?

How has God spoken to you in today's lesson? _____

_____

Lesson 5   Confusion or Clarification?
Day 4   James 2:23-24

5

Please read today's scripture in James 2:23-24 along with Romans 4:1-3.

Wait a minute! James tells us that we are justified by what we do and not by faith alone; then in Romans, Paul tells us that Abraham couldn't be justified by works, but he was credited as being righteous due to his belief in God. So which is it?

*First we need to understand the difference between the use of the words "justified" and "righteous." Justified is the **act** of being declared righteous (just-as-if-I'd never sinned); righteousness is the **state** of being right with God—in a right relationship. Second, we need to understand that God teaches with balance.*

In the book of Romans, Paul was writing to mainly Gentile Christians, however, Jewish Christians would be reading the letter as well. Gentiles were simply non-Jews who did not know or understand anything of the Jewish Old Testament teachings about the laws of God and the sacrifices for sin. Gentile Christians were taught to "Believe in the Lord Jesus Christ and you will be saved..." (Acts 16:31).

Because the foundational belief of Jews was obedience to the laws of God, the idea of being cleansed of sin by faith in Jesus Christ alone seemed incomplete; therefore, Jewish Christians were prone to add works as a means to secure their salvation. Meanwhile, Gentile Christians understood that their salvation was by faith alone in the sacrifice of Jesus--what else is needed? Both were right and yet, both were wrong as well.

Read Romans 4:4-5.

- How would you define "obligation?" _____

  _____

- What is the difference between giving a gift and a paycheck?_____

  _____

The difference is expectation. The Jewish Christians <u>expected</u> God to see them as righteous because of the works they added to their faith; the Gentile Christians didn't think God <u>expected</u> anything from them outside of their belief in Jesus Christ. It really comes down to a matter of the heart because from the outside, both actions look correct, don't they?

It would be easy to lose perspective on grace (unearned favor and love of God) through unbalanced thinking. The Jew would say, "I have to be very careful of losing God's grace by not doing the right things as a Christian." The Gentile would say, "I can sin all I want and ask for God's forgiveness because I automatically have his grace." God was addressing both extremes of thinking in both Romans and James.

Read Romans 4:18-22 and Hebrews 11:17-18.

- How was Abraham's life a balance between both faith and works?

  _____

  _____

- What was Abraham's ultimate belief in Romans 4:21? _____

- Abraham was called "God's friend" in James 2:23. Summarize the below verses that support the verse in James.

  2 Chronicles 20:7 _____

  Isaiah 41:8 _____

- What was the relationship between God and Moses like according to Exodus 33:11a?

  "The Lord would speak to Moses _____*, as a man*

  speaks _____ *."*

Wouldn't you just love to be known as God's friend?

- What are some of the characteristics of a friend according to the below verses in Proverbs?

  Proverbs 17:17a _____

  Proverbs 18:24b _____

  Proverbs 27:9b _____

Abraham loved God at all times; he stuck close to God even during the difficult times; he sought God's earnest counsel in his walk through life.

- Is God able to call you his friend? _____

  _____

A friend is someone you enjoy spending time with and they with you.

- What are some of the things you enjoy most about a friendship that you currently have?

  _____

  _____

- Do you enjoy spending time with God or is it more a sense of duty? _____

  _____

If your time with God seems more like a sense of duty rather than one of enjoyment, tell it to God. Be honest with him. It's not like he doesn't already know how you feel, right? Are you perhaps out of balance in your idea of grace? Maybe you're feeling like you always need to __do__ the right thing in order to have God's favor and love. There would be no enjoyment in that kind of relationship, would there?

*"He redeemed my soul from going down to the pit, and I will live to **enjoy the light**."*

Job 33:28

How has God spoken to you in today's lesson? _____

_____

It appears that James was scraping the bottom of the barrel in order to find examples of faith in action. Certainly he could have chosen a more fitting life to help drive home his point. So why on earth did he choose Rahab? A righteous prostitute; is there really such a thing? Isn't this a bit of an oxymoron? Let's take a closer look at the life of Rahab in the hopes that we might see from the perspective of James.

Please read James 2:25-26 along with Joshua 2:1-21.

- Why do you think the spies might have gone to the house of a prostitute?

  _____

- Rahab showed herself to be anything but timid. What were some of the actions that showed her boldness?

  _____

  _____

Rahab's bold actions came from a firm belief. In verse 9 Rahab said: "...I know that the Lord has given this land to you...."

- How did Rahab know this? _____

- What conclusion did she draw from this knowledge? (vs. 11) ___ _____ _____

  _____

Now that's a leap of faith! Rahab did not know God personally or have any kind of relationship with him; she heard about the power and might of God through word of mouth only, and yet, this belief prompted her to: (1) Lie to the King of Jericho, (2) Hide the spies, (3) Secretly let the spies out of her house by a rope through the window, (4) Proclaim "God is heaven above and on the earth below."

We can't help but wonder if Rahab remained a prostitute even after her profound confession of faith in God stated above. In God's word, she will forever be branded as "Rahab the prostitute." Was this truly who she remained?

- What else do we learn about the life of Rahab from the following verses?

    Joshua 6:22-25 _____

    Matthew 1:1-5 _____

    Hebrews 11:31 _____

Being known as "the prostitute" was not a judgment of Rahab's past life, but simply as a form of identification. After the Israelites conquered the city of Jericho, Rahab stayed living her life among the Israelites and walking with the God of heaven and earth. Rahab's faith is noted in both James and Hebrews. Not only that, her name is listed in the genealogy of Jesus simply as "Rahab." Did you catch that? Her identification had changed from being "the prostitute" to being a part of the lineage that birthed Jesus Christ. Wow! God redeemed Rahab's past life because of her faith.

- What about you? Has God been able to redeem your past life? If so, how?

    _____

    _____

- Is there anything that holds you back from allowing God to forgive and redeem you for things in the past?

    _____

    _____

- What was the one final action that was required of Rahab in order to protect her from death? (See Joshua 2:17-21)

    _____

Read Exodus 12:1-7, 12-13

- In what way is this story similar to that of Rahab? _____

    _____

John the Baptist, in seeing Jesus coming to him to be baptized, cried out, "Look, the Lamb of God, who takes away the sin of the world!" Jesus told his disciples that his blood would be poured out for many for the forgiveness of sins.

*In John 5:24 Jesus said: "I tell you the truth, whoever hears my word and believes him who sent me has eternal life and will not be condemned; he has crossed over from **death to life**."*

- Rahab crossed over from death to life because of her belief in God **along with** her action of tying the scarlet cord in her window.

- The Israelites crossed over from death to life because of their belief in God's word through Moses **along with** their action of placing the blood of a lamb on their doorposts.

- We cross over from death to life because of our belief in the sacrificial death of Jesus for our sins **along with** the actions of a life lived in obedience to the God of heaven above and earth below.

James sums up in 2:26: "As the body without the spirit is dead, so faith without deeds is dead."

The spirit gives life to the body and identifies who we are; our actions give life to our faith and identifies us as believers in Jesus.

How has God spoken to you in today's lesson? _____

_____

Lesson 6

James 3:1-12

Have you ever wanted to cut your tongue out over something you said that you knew could never be taken back? Have you tasted the bitterness of your foot in your mouth? Welcome to Club FIM (Foot in Mouth). Admission into the club is fairly simple: Are you breathing? Do you have a tongue? Can you speak audibly? Congratulations! You've made it into Club FIM!

*James must have been a member of Club FIM at one time because he was fully aware of the dangers of the tongue when he warned us to be "quick to listen, slow to speak and slow to become angry." He also reminded us that if we can't keep a tight rein on our tongues, then our religion was worthless. (Ouch! Remember that one?) He understood the reality that the tongue is the hardest part of the body to control. So, this week our eyes, ears and hearts will focus on various aspects of **the tongue**.*

Let's start by reading today's verses in James 3:1-2

Now before you quickly glance over this lesson thinking that it doesn't apply to you because you're not a teacher, don't be too quick to jump to that conclusion. Do you have children? Relatives? Christian friends and acquaintances? Then guess what, you're a teacher! You teach and instruct others each and every day through your words. What your words teach is another matter.

- Discuss the following examples of teaching with your words:

    Lie – "Tell them I'm not home."

    Hide truth – "Don't tell anyone…"

    Excuse wrong – "I'm tired, that's why I said it."

    Give thanks to God – "Let's tell God thank you for answering your prayer."

    Put God first – "We'll plan to do that after church on Sunday."

    Trust in God – "Yes, I lost my job, but God is faithful and will provide."

We can't be a teacher regarding the things of God without having first been a student. And if you desire to continually grow in God, you will always be a student at some level.

- Colossians 3:16 calls each one of us to teach. Read and discuss how this would look in everyday life.

    _____

    _____

    _____

During biblical times, the position of teacher was one of honor and value. Because of this, many aspired to become religious teachers whether they were morally qualified or not. Since Jesus could see into the hearts of men, He called out the motives of the religious leaders on their desire in becoming teachers.

- What motives did he expose in Mark 12:38-40? _____

- According to 1 Corinthians 8:1-2, what is the potential difficulty in having greater knowledge? _____

The ugly "P" word is P-R-I-D-E! James understood the motivating drive behind many who wanted to be religious teachers. James 3:1 reads like a prohibition to becoming a teacher, when in actuality he was making more of a suggestion. Why? Because teachers will be held to a greater accountability than others; they have a greater sphere of influence, and they stumble too (sin, make mistakes).

Representing God's character and truths accurately requires a discipline over our speech. We can't portray God as something we want Him to be when it isn't in line with His word. Our human nature wants to fit God's word into our belief system rather than the other way around.

- How about you? Do you ever find yourself trying to make God's word say what you want to hear in order to fit your lifestyle?

_____

*Everyone stumbles in one way or another (we're human after all); however, our speech is the most difficult aspect of the human life to control. James 3:2b says, "If anyone is **never** at fault in what he says, he is a **perfect** man, able to keep his whole body in check." Oh, good grief--never, perfect? We've heard many times to "Never say never," and "Only God is perfect." So what is James trying to say here?*

The essence of what he is saying in verse 2 is that you are a person who has withdrawn your membership from Club FIM because you have reached a level of maturity in your Christian life where the tongue no longer has control over you. <u>You</u> have control over it! Always? Of course not. There will be times when we are at fault in what we say; that's a result of our human nature. Becoming a "perfect" person is not one who is without sin, but rather one who knows, understands and lives according to the standards and principles of God's word--complete in God.

How has God spoken to you in today's lesson? _____

_____

In yesterday's lesson, we focused on the maturity of the tongue necessary in order to be an effective teacher of God's word. However, as we discovered yesterday, whether you have reached that level of maturity doesn't exclude you from the role of teacher. We teach about God each and every day through our actions and speech. Because you are reading these words and in a Bible study, the assumption is that you want to understand and apply the truths of God's word, right?

In today's verses, James uses some practical comparisons from everyday life to better help us understand the power the tongue has in directing our lives.

Read James 3:3-5

- What are the three comparisons James uses to emphasize the power of the tongue?

   _____

   _____

Let's focus on the example that James gave about the ship and the rudder. What exactly does verse 4 say?

- "Although they are so large and are _____ by strong winds, they are

   _____ by a very small _____ wherever the _____

   _____ _____ to _____."

Let's examine the analogy James uses?

- What do you think "driven by strong winds" refers to? _____

- What would the "small rudder" be? _____

- Who is the pilot who steers the rudder? _____

*Are you catching this? As women, we struggle with wanting control over people, places and things in our lives, don't we? The good news is that we **can** have complete control in one particular area of our lives--what we say.*

- What is the difference between something being "driven" vs. "steered?"

   _____

In looking up the definition of both, here's what we find:

Driven: To be carried, moved by force or compulsion.

Steered: "Directing the course of a vessel, vehicle, airplane, etc...by use of a rudder or other means."

Do you allow your tongue to be carried by the force of your strong emotions? Do any of the below sound familiar to you?

- Statement 1: "What goes around, comes around--she hurt me first."

- Statement 2: "I couldn't help myself......he just made me so mad."

- Statement 3: "I'm gonna tell it like it is."

It's clear that the above statements would earn us a lifetime membership to Club FIM, but what about the below? There's no foot in mouth here.

- Statement 4: "I really should say something, but they may not like me any longer."

- Statement 5: "I'll just keep quiet. I don't want to rock the boat."

Absolutely, there is no foot in mouth on these statements. But do you know what all five of these statements have in common? They are all driven by strong emotions. Whether the emotion is retaliation, anger, blunt honesty or the fear of rejection or confrontation, emotion is the driving force.

I hope you realize by now that God's word has direction and guidance for us in all areas of life. So let's see what God has to say regarding statements like the above from his book of wisdom, Proverbs.

Contrast each of the above statements with the below verses in Proverbs.

How would these verses help you steer your tongue in practical, everyday situations?

- Statement 1: Proverbs 12:16 _____

- Statement 2: Proverbs 11:12 _____

- Statement 3: Proverbs 13:3 _____

- Statement 4: Proverbs 16:13 _____

- Statement 5: Proverbs 28:23_____

What wisdom we can gain from God's word! We learn there is more value in a truthful rebuke than in words of flattery. When we learn to hold our tongue, look for the right timing to speak, and can overlook an insult done to us, we are guarding our lives--our character and reputation as a child of God.

Let's close today's lesson with two powerful proverbs on the tongue. What do you think Solomon meant in each of the below proverbs?

- Proverbs 18:20: *"From the fruit of his mouth a man's stomach is filled; with the harvest from his lips he is satisfied."*

_____

_____

- Proverbs 18:21: *"The tongue has the power of life and death, and those who love it will eat its fruit."*

_____

_____

How has God spoken to you in today's lesson? _____

_____

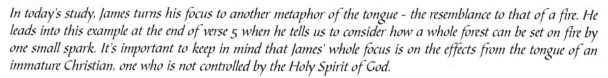

In today's study, James turns his focus to another metaphor of the tongue - the resemblance to that of a fire. He leads into this example at the end of verse 5 when he tells us to consider how a whole forest can be set on fire by one small spark. It's important to keep in mind that James' whole focus is on the effects from the tongue of an immature Christian, one who is not controlled by the Holy Spirit of God.

Read James 3:6

- What do you think James means when he says that the tongue is a "world of evil among the parts of the body?"

_____

_____

Generally speaking, there's nothing bad about the tongue; it's just an organ in the floor of our mouth that allows us to eat, taste and speak; any judgment as to whether the tongue is good or bad is based upon how a person chooses to use that particular instrument of their body. Our tongue represents which world we are living in at the time we speak; the world of God or the world of Satan (evil).

- What do we learn about the tongue and the nature of Satan in John 8:44?

_____

- How has Satan used your tongue to bring evil to life? _____

_____

James tells us that the tongue can corrupt the whole person. That's a strong statement when you consider some of the following definitions of "corrupt":

To mar, spoil, infect or taint; to lower morally, alter for the worse; to destroy the integrity of (honesty; sound moral character).

Does the tongue really have the power to do all this? Let's look at this with respect to the metaphor that James is using with regard to the tongue and fire.

- What three results of the tongue as a fire are used in James 3:6? _____

_____

Fire devours and destroys, injures beyond repair and can cause something to become ineffective or useless. In a nutshell, fire devastates!

- Based on the effects of fire (above) and some of the definitions of the word, "corrupt," how do you think the tongue can corrupt the whole person?

  _____

  _____

- How can the tongue set the whole course of a person's life on fire?

  _____

  _____

- How has the course of your life been changed due to something you said?

  _____

  _____

The uncontrolled fiery words we speak based on our emotions can injure another person beyond repair. Our thoughtless words can cause another to believe that they are ineffective or useless, having little or no value. Not only that, the words we use begin to corrupt us, infecting and causing us to morally lower our standards. Because our words are a mirror of our soul, such things as lies, gossip and backbiting destroy our integrity and cause people to view us as dishonest and lacking Godly character which then alters the course of our lives.

*We know that words spoken cannot be removed, but look up--there **is** hope!*

"Find rest, O my soul, in God alone; my hope comes from him." Psalm 62:5

Hope of what? 1 John 1:9 says, "If we confess our sins, he is faithful and just and will forgive us our sins and purify us from all unrighteousness." We have hope of forgiveness from God for hurtful words that we cannot take back.

Along with asking for God's forgiveness, God requires something else from us as well.

Please read Matthew 5:23-24

- Summarize these verses in your own words. _____

  _____

There is often more to righting a wrong than just asking for forgiveness from God. Right now, seek God in truth asking him if there is someone you need to ask forgiveness from because of your out-of-control tongue.

- Has God revealed someone to you? _____

- Now here's the million-dollar question: What will you do with this?

  _____

How has God spoken to you in today's lesson? _____

_____

Are you feeling a bit tempted right now to perform your own tongue-ectomy and get rid of that flabby piece of flesh in your mouth that causes so much trouble? You're probably not alone in that feeling.

"If only..........I hadn't said that."

"If only..........I could do it over again."

"If only..........I could take it back."

James isn't really much help in today's lesson as he piles on more ugliness with regards to the tongue. The "Reality Bites" slogan is being stretched to the limit here, isn't it?

Let's read James 3:7-8 together.

- What three stinging remarks does James use to point out the reality of the tongue in today's verses?

  _____

  _____

Does a circus come to your mind when you hear the phrase "have been tamed?" That's not quite the picture James is attempting to draw here. We know there are untamed animals roaming all over the world (you may have one or two living in your own homes). So what does he mean?

- How does Genesis 1:26 add clarity to what James is saying?_____

  _____

James is speaking about the authority God gave to man to dominate and restrain His creatures. We can exercise restraint over animals but not our own tongues! We're probably all thinking the same thing about now; why bother then if the tongue can't be tamed? Hold that thought, because we'll talk more about that a bit later.

- What do you think James is trying to teach when he says the tongue is a "restless evil?"

  _____

We all know what it feels like to be restless, don't we? But when we relate it to the tongue, ouch-- it hurts! A restless tongue is one that is always in motion, unceasingly active and never at rest. We leave the door wide open for evil to enter.

- How does Proverbs 10:19a expand on this idea? _____

  _____

Lesson 6
Day 4

Who Controls Your Tongue?
James 3:7-8

6

- How does Proverbs 12:18a add additional insight? _____

_____

Do you know what it means to be reckless? It means to be utterly unconcerned about the consequences of an action. The more we talk, the less time we have to think before we speak and use caution before we open our mouths. The result is that our words can pierce another person like a sword. Wow! That's a lot of power in one mouth! Not only that, the tip of that sword is full of deadly poison (as James points out) which means that our words can be deadly.

Read Deuteronomy 29:18

- What produces bitter poison? _____

Anything that you focus the majority of your thoughts, time and energy on can become your "god." We serve a jealous God who doesn't want other people or things to be more important than him. After all, he created us for relationship with Him. When our hearts turn from God, roots begin to grow in our hearts that produce bitter poison. Tomorrow, we will focus our attention on the heart and how it relates to our tongues.

*So, the question was asked earlier: "Why bother then if the tongue can't be tamed?" Did you catch when James said that? "No **man** can tame the tongue." He never said that it couldn't be tamed; just that man couldn't tame it. Are you one step ahead of the thinking? Man can't, BUT GOD CAN!*

Let's turn and read Romans 8:9 together

- Summarize this verse in your own words. _____

_____

_____

What does it mean to be "controlled by the spirit?" To control something is to subdue it; to conquer it and bring it into subjection; to overpower with superior force; to bring it under mental or emotional control. If God's spirit is truly controlling us, He can tame our tongues. There is one little catch here, God doesn't force us under His control; He only takes control as we give it to Him. We have to exercise self-control over our sin nature in order to allow God's spirit to take control.

Read Romans 8:1-8

- What is the common theme of these verses? _____

6

Who Controls Your Tongue?
James 3:7-8

Lesson 6
Day 4

In order to exercise control over our sin nature, we have to mentally choose to be controlled by God's spirit; that's where the self-control comes into play.

- Summarize and discuss verse 5 _____

    _____

- Colossians 3:2 tells us to set our minds on things above. How can we do that? (See Romans 8:5-6)

    _____

- What three urgent pieces of advice does Peter give us in 1 Peter 1:13?

    _____

*We have to prepare our minds to actively surrender our will (sin nature) over to the control of God. We cannot do this unless we discipline ourselves to do the very things that go against our natural desires. Let's face it, ultimately, we want our way and not God's way. The only way we can do any of this is by keeping our perspective on eternity versus now. Jesus Christ **will** return; He **will** be revealed.*

"So we fix our eyes not on what is seen, but on what is unseen. For what is seen is temporary, but what is unseen is eternal."

2 Corinthians 4:18

How has God spoken to you in today's lesson? _____

_____

We've been dissecting the various aspects of the tongue all week, and it hasn't been pleasant, has it? We've come to realize that we all teach others through the words we use every single day. When we let our emotions rule, our tongue becomes an out-of-control instrument for evil that can destroy others and change the course of our lives. We know that God chooses to limit His ability to guide and guard our tongues until we exercise self-control over our sin nature and surrender to God so that we can be Spirit-controlled.

The one key question that hasn't been addressed yet is the "why"? Why do I say the things I do? Why does my tongue run away with me? Why do I continually hurt others with my words when I really don't want to? The answer to those questions is in the heart behind the tongue.

Read James 3:9-12

With the same tongue we praise God and curse others made in God's image. How can this be? James asks a question of his readers in vs. 11, "Can both fresh water and salt water flow from the same spring?"

- How would you answer this question? _____

    _____

- In looking at Isaiah 29:13, what did God view as the problem?_____

    _____

It can be said that the best indicators of a person's true character come out during times of storms or times of calm. Do you really want to know what a person believes in their heart? Watch that person during a time of crisis, or go ask their close family (where they are the most comfortable), and you will get a fuller understanding of the character of that person.

- What does 1 Samuel 16:7b say? "Man looks at the outward appearance, but the Lord

    _____

    _____ ."

We know that only God sees the heart of a person, but Jesus did teach His disciples to be alert as to what comes out of a person's mouth because it's an indicator of the condition of his or her heart.

- Summarize what Jesus had to say in Matthew 15:16-20._____

    _____

- What insights do you gain about God and the heart from Jeremiah 17:9-10?

_____

_____

Listen to what David said in Psalm 139:23-24:

"Search me, O God, and know my heart; test me and know my anxious thoughts; see if there is any offensive way in me, and lead me in the way everlasting."

Have you ever allowed God to perform heart surgery on you? Have you ever opened yourself completely to Him and asked Him to show you those things within you that are offensive to Him and holding you back from a deeper relationship with Him and others?

Right now, why not put down your pencil and spend some quiet time with God on this matter of the heart. He is faithful and will lovingly and truthfully show you those areas that need His touch. Remember, you aren't hiding anything from Him anyway, right? He already knows your heart inside and out. Write out some of your personal thoughts below (for your eyes only).

_____

_____

James used the analogy of fruit from the fig tree and the grapevine--fig trees can't produce grapes any more than grapevines can produce figs. A tree is known by its fruit.

- What point is Jesus making in Luke 6:43-45? _____

_____

- What is the "fruit" that Jesus is referring to? (Galatians 5:22-23) _____

_____

Read John 15:1-8

- Who is the gardener and what is his role?_____

- Who is the vine and what is his role? _____

- Who are the branches and what is their role? _____

  _____

- What do you think Jesus means when he says, "Remain in me?" _____

  _____

A vital, living everyday relationship with Jesus is the only way we will ever get control over our tongue. In order to let God take the driver's seat, we will have to surrender our will (sin nature) over to Him which will allow us to be Spirit controlled. Remember that our "fruit" comes from His Spirit; the more Spirit controlled we are, the more fruit we will produce.

From the fruit of his mouth, a man's stomach is filled; with the harvest from his lips he is satisfied.

Proverbs 18:20

How has God spoken to you in today's lesson? _____

_____

Notes

Lesson 7

James 3:13-18

James has been relentless in his pursuit to help us understand that without action, there is no faith; without action, there is no wisdom; without action, there is no understanding. Faith, wisdom and understanding are empty words if there is no accompanying action showing our belief.

Read today's verse in James 3:13

Are any of you wise and understanding? Great! It's going to show by the kind of life you live and in the humility surrounding your actions. But what kind of wisdom is James talking about here? There appear to be two types of wisdom in Scripture, so let's try and make sure we are on the same page with James as to his meaning of wisdom.

Please read 1 Corinthians 1:20-25, 30

- What two types of wisdom do you see? _____

- What is the main idea that Paul is trying to convey in these verses?

  _____

  _____

- How is Christ our "wisdom from God?" _____

  _____

A crucified Christ is God's wisdom? How can that be? In looking through the eyes of human wisdom, it's absolute foolishness, isn't it? But we're called to look through different eyes.

Read 1 Corinthians 2:11-14

- What is the key to understanding God's wisdom? _____

Wisdom is defined as the ability to judge what is true, right or lasting; to discern. How can we possibly discern the ways and wisdom of God without the Spirit of God living within us? It's impossible! We are warned in

1 Thessalonians not to "put out the Spirit's fire." If we ignore the Spirit's presence in our lives (His leading and guidance) and choose to willfully sin, we have effectively drowned out His voice in our lives. Oh, He's still there, but His voice is being ignored.

We are told by James that humility is a by-product that comes from having wisdom and understanding. But before we can understand what "deeds done in humility" look like, we need to first take a look at the actions required of us in order to attain wisdom and understanding.

What actions do the following verses require towards the pursuit of wisdom and understanding?

- Proverbs 2:2 _____

- Proverbs 4:5 _____

- Proverbs 4:7 _____

Wisdom comes at a cost--everything you have. Acquiring wisdom will require a completely open heart before God in order for Him to begin to teach you His truths that you can begin to apply to your life. This is done through a continual pursuit of His word that will ultimately show up in the kind of life you live--one of humility.

Unfortunately, humility is one of those characteristics that only shows up when you aren't aware of it. If someone asks you if you consider yourself to be humble, and you answer "yes," you've just shot down the whole meaning and heart of what true humility is.

A humble person is one who is not proud or arrogant; it's a person who is aware of their own lack of importance and significance in the big picture of life; it is someone who is submissive and respectful. We've seen that wisdom from God comes from knowing Jesus Christ. Not coincidentally, our example of humility is also shown best in the life of Jesus.

- Read Matthew 11:28-30. What does Jesus want us to learn from Him?

  _____

He invites us to learn humility through the example of His life. Undoubtedly, the best example we have on the humility of Jesus is found in Philippians.

Please read Philippians 2:5-11.

Let's break this down a bit into bite-sized pieces in order to get a fuller understanding.

- Read and summarize verses 5-7 _____

  _____

  _____

- Read and summarize verse 8. _____

_____

- Read and summarize verses 9-11. _____

_____

Jesus' essential form is the total of the very qualities that make God specifically God. Jesus shared the glory, status and privileges that follow from being in very nature God. let go of his   H Since they were already His, He didn't feel the need to grab hold of His position and authority but willingly gave them up. eHeHHe He "made himself nothing." In humility, He set aside His privileges and glory as God.

Think about this for a minute. He chose to step down from heaven and put on the body of His own creation; He submitted Himself as a servant under the authority of the very people He created; in complete dependence He drew all His power and strength from His Heavenly Father and then willingly allowed Himself to be executed in the most degrading kind of way--crucifixion.

Jesus allowed Himself to appear to be insignificant to those around Him in absolute and complete humility. To the human eye, this is foolishness. Christ is our wisdom from God? How? Where is God's wisdom in all this? Maybe we'll find it if we read on a bit more:

"Therefore God exalted him to the highest place and gave him the name that is above every name,

That at the name of Jesus every knee should bow, in heaven and on earth and under the earth,

And every tongue confess that Jesus Christ is Lord to the glory of God the Father."

There it is! Do you see it? Look hard and with spiritual eyes because "we live by faith, not by sight." 2 Corinthians 5:7.

- What do you think Jesus meant in Matthew11:19b when He said, "Wisdom is proved right by her actions?"

_____

_____

*The results of applying God's wisdom aren't always immediately evident. Sometimes, it can take years to see the rightness of the actions we've taken in obedience to God's word.   But Jesus didn't say that wisdom **might be** proved right by her actions or **will hopefully be,** He confidently said, "Wisdom **is** proved right by her actions."*

How has God spoken to you in today's lesson? _____

_____

Read James 3:14

At first glance, it appears that we are making a big shift today. From Godly wisdom, understanding and humility, it looks like we're heading in a completely different direction. Or is it? Take a look at that little word "but" that starts the beginning of verse 14. James is going to contrast true wisdom which is evidenced by Godly living with another kind of so-called wisdom. Today we are going to focus on the specifics of this "other wisdom" (envy, selfish ambition and boasting), and tomorrow we will look deeper into the source of this so-called wisdom.

The context of verse 14 doesn't seem to make much sense, does it? If you were envious or had selfish ambition, would you boast about it to others? You might deny the truth of those feelings within yourself, but boast about them? Of course not! Well then, there must be more to this than meets the eye.

*In reference to boasting, James says, "...do not boast about **it**." What is "it?" Since there isn't a subject matter given, we have to look back to verse 13 to find the subject-- Godly wisdom. Maybe it looks something like this:*

> "I want what she has (bitter envy). It isn't fair, she has a close relationship with God; she's always doing the right thing and God seems to bless her life. Everyone looks up to her and likes her. I want people to look up to me like that (selfish ambition); I'm going to start telling people (boasting) that I have God's wisdom too, so they'll start looking up to me like they do her."

Read Mark 15:1-15

- What was the result of envy according to these verses? _____

- Why do you think the religious leaders were envious of Jesus? (See Matt. 23-1-7)

  _____

  _____

The bitter envy of the religious leaders led them to hand this innocent man Jesus over to be crucified. They thought that would be the end of their problem. But we know that "wisdom is proved right by her actions." God knew what He was doing in spite of the actions of the religious leaders. Isn't it a good feeling to know that God's in charge and in complete control of any and every situation?

- Can you share a time when you struggled with envy? Are you still struggling?

  _____

  _____

We need to keep in mind that everything James has been addressing from day one is to people within the church. They were Christians just like us who had difficulty in their faith, struggled with doubt and temptations, had trouble holding their tongues, allowed pride to rule, and were driven by their selfish ambitions. We are not alone in our faith journey; others have gone before us.

Is ambition bad? Isn't ambition just having goals or aims, a desire for work or activity?

- In Romans 15:20, Paul shared his ambition. What was it? _____

Maybe ambition just becomes bad when the word "selfish" is placed in front of it; then it becomes a strong desire to achieve something like power, honor, fame or wealth and being willing to do everything to get it. The focus becomes ME, ME, ME!

Read Philippians 2:1-4

- From verse 2, in what three ways would Paul's joy be made complete?

  _____

- How would this look in church when everyone has different opinions, ideas and thoughts? Must everyone think alike in order to have unity?

  _____

  _____

Unity within the church, within families, or with friends can never happen when our focus is on us--selfish ambition and vain conceit.

- What do you think Paul meant when he said, "...in humility, consider others better than yourselves"?

  _____

  _____

Humility is simply the realization that the world doesn't revolve around us; it's understanding our place and importance within the bigger picture; it's having a right attitude about ourselves. It's not that everyone else is better than us or more talented, but because we are united with Christ, we see them as worthy of special treatment.

- (Personal) Who's the center of your universe? _____

  _____

If truth be told, I'm sure we're all guilty of a little boasting (bigging ourselves up when we feel intimidated or overshadowed), but what about those who seem to have no limits? You know who they are. We've all met the boaster, the person in the room who can't wait to tell us all how fantastic they are and how they are good at this and even better at that. Whatever subject is introduced, they know everything about it. Without doubt, they can be exhausting, but what exactly is behind the boasting?

- Why do you think people boast? _____

_____

If we boast to somehow make ourselves look better or more important, maybe that's the problem--our own self esteem. If we see ourselves as lower or less than others, we are more likely to take offense where there is none; perhaps we read into things and become highly sensitive to any hint of criticism. Worst of all, we won't hear or will discount any compliments or praise that are directed towards us because we have an automatic filter that hears only the negative. This would naturally impact our thinking on how God views us as well.

- According to Isaiah 43:3-4, how are we viewed by God?_____

- Do you have trouble believing this? Why? _____

_____

Walking in faith means taking God at His word. It means choosing to believe that His promises are true because He is absolute truth--He cannot lie. You are precious and honored because He said so. Period. No exceptions. Regardless of what you have done in your life, good or bad, He loves you because you are His beloved creation.

- What can we boast about according to Jeremiah 9:23-24? _____

_____

Boasting, like all other actions of the tongue, come from within our heart. When we know and believe our value and worth in the eyes of God, we don't feel the need to boast in order to elevate ourselves in the eyes of others. But if we truly know and understand God, we can't help but boast about Him to others, shouting out about His love, kindness, justice and righteousness. Our boasting will bubble forth out of a heart of love.

How has God spoken to you in today's lesson? _____

_____

The "wisdom" that James addresses today is really not wisdom at all, but is used to show the stark contrast between living in Godly wisdom and living without Godly wisdom. This so-called wisdom does not come down from heaven. We were told in James 1:17 that "Every good and perfect gift is from God above, coming down from the Father of the heavenly lights...." Envy and selfish ambition could not in any way be considered good gifts; they don't originate in heaven (from God); and we're told they are earthly, unspiritual and of the devil.

Let's read James 3:15-16

It's interesting that envy and selfish ambition are the focal characteristics of these verses of which James clearly states are from the devil; these characteristics originate from Satan. In order to help us understand a bit more about the person they come from, we're going to look at two scriptures in Isaiah and Ezekiel. These verses have a two-fold meaning: Isaiah is stating God's judgment of the current king of Babylon while Ezekiel's words are judgment against the king of Tyre. The underlying meaning of both of these verses is the history and condemnation of Satan, Lucifer, the morning star.

Read Isaiah 14:12-14 and Read Ezekiel 28:12-17

- In what ways do you see pride and selfish ambition at work in Satan?

  _____

- List some of the things you learned about Satan from these verses._____

  _____

  _____

- What additional things do you learn about Satan in 1 John 3:8-9 & 5:18-19?

  _____

Satan has been sinning from the beginning, from the time he first rebelled against God before the fall of Adam and Eve. He is the instigator of all human sin and has the entire world of unbelievers under his control.

1 John 3:8 tells us that the reason the Son of God appeared was to "destroy the devil's work." The question we can't help but ask is, "What is the devil's work?" Let's go back to James 3 and take another look.

- What works of Satan do we find when there is envy and selfish ambition?

  _____

*So we see in the Devil's work disorder and **every** evil practice. The definition of "disorder" is: confusion; breach of order. And what's the definition of "breach?" It's violation as of law, trust, faith or promise. Job 25:2 says, "Dominion and awe belong to God; He establishes order in the heights of heaven."*

So then, we could say that disorder is the violation of God's created order with regards to His law, trust, faith and promises.

Read Romans 1:18-25

- How is God's creative order shown in these verses? _____

_____

- What evidences do you see of disorder? _____

- Why did God "give them over" to every evil practice? ___ _____

_____

Read Romans 1:26-32

- What are some of the evil practices listed that stand out the most to you?

_____

We've been talking this week about Godly wisdom and the contrast with this "other wisdom" (which, as we've seen is really not wisdom at all). The book of Proverbs uses comparison and contrast as a means of teaching. In Proverbs, those who don't exercise wisdom are considered fools.

- What do the following say regarding the wise and foolish?

Proverbs 10:23 _____

Proverbs 12:15 _____

Proverbs 13:16 _____

Re-read Romans 1:21-23

Why were their foolish hearts darkened? _____

- How did they become fools? _____

Were you able to grasp the contrast between the proverbs listed above and the foolishness of mankind listed in Romans?

*Proverbs 13 says that a wise (prudent) man acts out of knowledge; Romans; 1:21 says, "For although they **knew** God, they neither glorified him as God nor gave thanks to him, but their **thinking** became futile (ineffective) and their foolish hearts were darkened."*

*Proverbs 10 states that a man of understand delights in wisdom but a fool finds pleasure in evil conduct; Romans 1:24 says, "Therefore, God gave them over in **the sinful desires of their hearts**...."*

*Proverbs 12 reminds us that the way of a fool seems right to him, but a wise man listens to advice; Romans 1:32 says, "Although they know God's righteous decree that those who do such things deserve death, **they not only continue to do these very things but also approve of those who practice them**."*

How has God spoken to you in today's lesson? _____

_____

Yesterday, we were given a vivid picture in Romans of what a life without God and His wisdom looks like--complete chaos and disorder shown by an ungodly lifestyle. We know from James 3:13 that Godly wisdom and understanding are evidenced by the kind of life we live and the attitude in which we live that life--one of humility. Today, James highlights the qualities of a life lived in Godly wisdom.

Read James 3:17

James states first and foremost that the wisdom that comes from heaven is pure. It is the exact opposite of "every evil practice." This wisdom is free from contamination; it's innocent and untainted with evil. Let's look at a few other benefits of Godly wisdom before we move on to the qualities of this wisdom.

Read Proverbs 2:1-15

- In order to acquire Godly wisdom, what are some of the actions we must take?

  _____

  _____

- We're told wisdom will be our shield; it will guard and protect us. What do you think we need protecting from?

  _____

- Verse 11 says, "Discretion will protect you, and understanding will guard you." How do you think discretion and understanding can guard and protect you?

  _____

  _____

We know that wisdom is the ability to judge what is true, right or lasting--discernment according to the standards of God. It's also important for us to remember that this ability to judge and discern God's ways is not something we can do on our own.

- Summarize 1 Corinthians 2:13 in your own words. _____

  _____

God's ways are revealed to us by His Spirit. Our faith doesn't rest on our own wisdom, but on God's power working in and through us (1 Corinthians 2:5). We can know and understand the thoughts of God because, when we belong to Him, we have His Spirit living and working within us. Amen!

In looking back to James, the pure qualities of Godly wisdom are: peace-loving, considerate, submissive, full of mercy and good fruit, impartial and sincere. As you read these qualities, are you giving yourself mental grades as to how well you do in these various areas? Well, don't! Remember, we are our own worst critics.

Let's explore what these qualities would look like in the life of a child of God in relationship to others; and then, with whole-hearted permission, allow God to speak to your heart regarding any of these individual areas in your life. Then write down your prayer to God in that particular area(s).

- **Peace-loving.** Let's start with what this doesn't mean. It doesn't mean never rocking the boat, never sharing your views or opinions if they differ from someone else's. Peace-loving is the exact opposite of quarrelsome. Do you make an issue out of everything? Using a familiar expression, do you make mountains out of molehills? If so, why? Is there a need to always be right or appear right? Does everything have to become an issue?

Dear God: _____

_____

- **Considerate.** Remember in Philippians 2:3, "...*but in humility* **consider others** *better than ourselves.*" Do you ever consider others? Are you aware of the needs, circumstances and feelings of others, or do you bounce through life unaware of anything outside your own immediate world?

Being considerate is characterized by deliberate, careful thought. For example, a friend <u>noticed</u> that her friend was sick, so she went home, made a pot of chicken noodle soup and brought it over to her friend. She looked around and <u>saw a need</u>, gave <u>careful thought</u> to what she could do to help, <u>deliberately</u> set aside time to make a pot of soup, and delivered it to her friend's house. That is what being considerate looks like in action.

Dear God: _____

_____

- **Submissive.** Of course, we immediately think of the submission of a wife to her husband, and our blood pressure starts to go up! Yes, God has established a chain of authority regarding man and woman, but it's not a chain of superiority. The idea of submission in the context of these verses is one of military troops under the control of a commander; it's a willingness to yield to others.

We are called to submit to authority every single day through the government, employers, teachers, organizations, financial institutions – not just to our husbands.

1 Peter 2:13 tells us to *"submit to every authority instituted by man for the Lord's sake."* If we can't submit to earthly authority that God has put in place, how can we ever say we submit to God? For an understanding of how submission looks, we must turn to the example of Jesus.

Read Matthew 26:36-42. Jesus endured painful submission to the point of death; and yet he trusted in His Father. *"Yet not as I will, but as you will."*

Dear God: _____

_____

• **Mercy and good fruit.** What do the following verses say about fruit?

Matthew 3:8 _____

Matthew 7:20 _____

Philippians 1:9-11 _____

When we repent from our sins and begin living a life of righteousness through Jesus (because we now have a right relationship with Him), people will recognize us as followers of Jesus because of the fruit we produce in our lives (our words and actions). The fruit of the spirit is love, joy, peace, patience, kindness, goodness, faithfulness, gentleness and self-control. (Galatians 5:22-23)

What are you producing?

Dear God: _____

_____

• **Sincere.** We've discussed impartiality and prejudice in previous lessons, so let's focus on what it means to be sincere. To be sincere is to be without hypocrisy; free of deceit or falseness. Hypocrisy is pretending to have a virtuous character based on moral or religious beliefs or principles that one does not really possess.

Do you act one way at home and another way at church?; one way around certain friends and another way around "church" friends? At home, do you live what you say you believe, or is it something different? To be sincere is to be genuine, no pretense. You are who you are regardless of the circumstance or situation.

- **Dear God:** _____

_____

Did you ever think there would be so many aspects to wisdom and so many ways that it can be shown? James does an outstanding job in contrasting God's wisdom from the wisdom of the world (well, we'll call it "wisdom" for lack of a better definition). On our final day of our focus on God's wisdom, we are going to look at the concept of peacemaking.

- How would you define a peacemaker? _____

  _____

The true definition of a peacemaker is a mediator; someone who tries to make peace by reconciling people who are in disagreement or conflict with one another. It's something like that of a marriage counselor. More often than not, though, we won't be acting as a third-party peacemaker because we're usually smack dab in the middle of the conflict either as the offender or the offended.

*Too often our idea of "peace" is to just ignore the person or situation altogether. We may give them the ever-popular silent treatment or the tried-and-true cold shoulder; but that is **not** the kind of peacemaker that James is talking about.*

Romans 12:18 says, "If it is possible, <u>as far as it depends on you</u>, live at peace with everyone."

- What do you think this means? _____

  _____

Being a peacemaker requires effort, action and <u>determination</u> on our part. While we have no control as to whether the other person will accept our offer of peace, we still have the responsibility to offer peace.

- From the following verses, what practical action could you take in order to be a peacemaker?

  Proverbs 19:11 _____

  Matthew 5:23-24 _____

  Ephesians 4:26 _____

The reality is that God brings situations and people into our lives to expose our sin-- ouch! The question is what do you do when you're exposed. Do you defend, justify and excuse your actions, or do you use the opportunity to allow God to "grow you" in that particular area? Growing may require apologizing to someone, attempting to reconcile a broken relationship or perhaps forgiving a hurt.

Is God bringing someone to your mind as you read this where He wants you to act as a peacemaker? Prayerfully ask Him what steps you need to take in order to be a peacemaker.

- (Personal) Share with your group and ask for prayer in taking this step in loving obedience to God.

James uses an analogy of planting and harvesting (sowing and reaping) with regards to peace. "Peacemakers who sow in peace raise a harvest of righteousness."

Read Galatians 6:7-9

These are some power-packed verses. We have a warning, contrast, encouragement and a promise all in these two verses.

- Why do you think we're being warned against deception in verse 7?

  _____

- What are the contrasts of reaping and sowing in verse 8? _____

  _____

- What encouragement and promise does verse 8 offer us?_____

  _____

Isn't it interesting that we're warned about self-deception with regards to sowing and reaping? And then "God cannot be mocked" is thrown in there. It makes a bit more sense when we understand what it means to be "mocked." To mock someone is to challenge or defy them; to treat them with ridicule or contempt.

Throughout God's word we are challenged and called to live what we believe and to put feet to our faith with action. The book of Proverbs reminds us over and over again about the law of choices and consequences. Listen to Proverbs 11:18:

> *"The wicked man earns deceptive wages, but he who sows righteousness reaps a sure reward."*

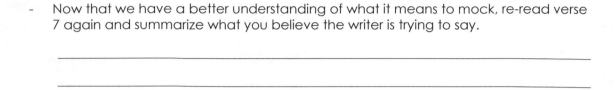
- Now that we have a better understanding of what it means to mock, re-read verse 7 again and summarize what you believe the writer is trying to say.

_____

_____

Romans 10:9 says, "If you confess with your mouth, 'Jesus is Lord,' and believe in your heart that God raised him from the dead, you will be saved." And yet, we've all heard people say that they know they are going to heaven because they are "good people" even though they don't believe in Jesus Christ; He is not their Lord, but they believe they will go to heaven anyway based upon nothing but their own hope.

Choosing to believe in our own made-up truth outside the truth of God's word is to show contempt for God. In essence, it's challenging God's truth and saying, "I'll live by my own standards and still go to heaven." This is what it means to mock God. Anytime we pick and choose from God's word what we will and will not believe is defying God-- mocking Him.

Did you notice that it doesn't say "God <u>will not allow himself</u> to be mocked" but it says, "God <u>cannot</u> be mocked." Just because lightening doesn't come down and strike us when we live outside of God's truth doesn't mean that we have somehow gotten away with something or God just didn't notice. God cannot be defied; His word is truth. As our creator, His laws are just, true and constant. You've heard the expression, "What goes around comes around." Well, that's really just another way of saying that we'll reap what we sow.

James tells us that if we sow in peace, we'll raise a harvest of righteousness.

- According to Hebrews 12:11, what are we trained in and what does it produce?

_____

God's discipline teaches and trains us to live within the wisdom of His word. It's not always comfortable; sometimes it's even painful because it can be the direct opposite of what we naturally want to do. However, we are promised a harvest of righteousness if we stay the course.

- How has God spoken to you in today's lesson? _____

_____

Notes

Lesson 8

James 4:1-10

James is showing the single-mindedness of his thoughts and direction in his approach to the problems going on inside the church at the time of this letter. He's identified and addressed their evil desires, lust, self-deception, anger, moral filth, deadly tongues, bitter envy and selfish ambitions. (He sure knows how to "call 'em as he sees 'em," doesn't he?) He goes on to say that all their sin is causing fights and quarrels among them and disorder within the church body.

In our lessons today and tomorrow we are going to see a much harsher and more confrontational James than we have previously. He now takes them to the bottom line: the core of their spiritual problem is their overpowering desire and craving for gratification, lust and evil pleasures.

Please read James 4:1-3

James identifies a "battle within." The NASB states it the following way: "Is not the source your pleasures that **wage war** *in your members?" Paul identified this battle in a very direct manner.*

- According to Romans 7:21-23, what is the battle? _____

  _____

- How can you relate to this internal battle? _____

  _____

It's interesting because the word "battle" implies two opposing sides fighting, and yet it appears from verse 2 of James that they aren't even fighting against their evil desires.

James answers his rhetorical question in verse 1 with a cause-and-effect relationship between evil desires and the resulting fights and quarrels. The NASB shows this parallel more clearly:

Cause	Effect
You lust and do not have;	*you commit murder.*
You are envious and cannot obtain;	*you fight and quarrel.*

Lust parallels envy; "do not have" parallels "cannot obtain;" "you commit murder" parallels "you fight and quarrel."

- Going back to James 1:14-15, what did he have to say about our lust (evil desire) and its result?

  _____

If we read James 4:2 as written, it appears that our lustful, evil desires can cause us to commit murder, and that murder is synonymous with fighting and quarreling. Is that what he really means? Let's look at a teaching from Jesus on murder.

Read Matthew 5:21-22

- According to Jesus, what did he equate to murder? _____

- Is anger really the same as murder? What point do you think Jesus was trying to make?

  _____

James is using the same figurative style of teaching as Jesus did on this point in order to make a direct hit.

- According to Matthew 15:18-19, what is the central point both Jesus and James are making?

  _____

  _____

It's <u>always</u> a "heart matter" where God is concerned, isn't it? If you're full of anger, you can effectively "murder" someone with your tongue. In God's eyes, there's no difference. 1 Chronicles 28:9 says: "...for the Lord searches every heart and understands every motive behind the thoughts." There's no pretending with God!

- In what way is God speaking to you this very moment? _____

  _____

It's a bit baffling that after James confronts the intense desire, craving and lust for pleasure, he states simply at the end of verse 2 that they don't have because they don't ask God. As if to say, "All you have to do is ask God if you have a desire; stop fighting and quarreling about it." However, let's remember the spiritual condition of the church to which he's writing; they've stopped talking to God about much of anything. Their lack of prayer is based on the simple fact that they no longer desire the things of God.

Maybe some of you remember the old Snicker's commercial that said, "It's so satisfying." Snickers, the great mid-afternoon pick-me-up; it will take your blood sugar sky high, and then send it crashing down so you feel worse than before. Satisfying? Hardly.

In a sense, that's exactly what was happening to these people; they were looking to satisfy their desires outside of God--the only real source of satisfaction and fulfillment. Does this ring a bell with any of you? It certainly rang a bell with Solomon as we will see from the following verses.

Please read Ecclesiastes 2:1-11

- List some of the things that Solomon sought in his quest for satisfaction.

  _____

  _____

- What are some of the ways you've looked for satisfaction outside of God?

  _____

- What conclusion did Solomon come to in verse 11? _____

Let's put a placeholder here for a second and go back to James. He seems to contradict himself between the end of verse 2 and verse 3. First he says that they don't ask; then he says that they ask with wrong motives and for their own pleasure. "Oh, God, please bless me with a new house...car...job...more money....." "I promise God, I'll use it for you." (Remember, God searches every heart and understands every motive.)

When our prayers become a time of selfishly asking God for things to satisfy our own cravings and desires outside of God, it's as if we haven't prayed at all. Since God's ultimate desire is to draw us closer to Him and to find satisfaction in Him, He will not hand us things that will even temporarily cause us to find satisfaction outside of Him; His desire for our spiritual good is first and foremost in His heart and actions towards us.

Solomon came to the conclusion that everything in life was meaningless outside of God. What about you? Are you still looking to fit the round peg in the square hole?

Listen to the words of Isaiah 55:2:

> "Why spend money on what is not bread, and your labor on what does not satisfy? Listen, listen to me, and eat what is good, and your soul will delight in the richest of fare."

How has God spoken to you in today's lesson? _____

_____

James loads his gun again today and aims a shot straight at the heart. He fires off words like "adulterous," "hatred," "enemy" and "intense envy." He effectively turns the tables on his readers; he confronted their envy for the things they wanted but couldn't have along with their pleasure-seeking motives, and then he states that the spirit God caused to live in us envies intensely or jealously desires as the NASB states. God gets jealous? Isn't that sin? But...God can't sin, right?

Let's read today's verses in James 4:4-5

Isn't it interesting that James calls his readers "adulterous?" When did adultery all of a sudden enter the picture, and how on earth does this apply? Why does being a friend of the world mean hatred toward God and make us an enemy of God?

- What do you think it means to be a "friend of the world?" _____

  _____

- What do the following verses say about the world?

  Ephesians 2:1-3 _____

  1 John 2:16 _____

The ways of the world cause us to follow our sinful cravings, desires and thoughts; our lusts and boasting of our accomplishments and possessions do not come from God but from the world. Ultimately, to follow the ways of the world is to follow Satan, the ruler of the kingdom of the air.

- What does Jesus say in Luke 11:23? _____

Jesus couldn't have put it any simpler, could He? Just as there is no such thing as being a little pregnant (either we are or we aren't), there is no such thing as "sort of" following God; we are either for Him or against Him; there's no middle ground. We show hatred or hostility towards God when we <u>choose</u> to follow the ways of this world rather than God's principles and commands. We <u>make ourselves</u> enemies of God when we <u>choose</u> to become actively hostile to the ways of God for the ways of the world.

Before you start thinking that because you still sin you must be choosing the things of the world and be against God, let's make sure we are keeping this in perspective.

- Summarize 1 John 1:8-9 in your own words. _____

_____

God planned ahead! He knew we would still sin, and made provision to forgive and cleanse us when we confess our sins to Him. It's not about never sinning again, but it's about the heart and attitude behind the sin. James is addressing those with the willful desire to live outside God's commands and principles and choosing to follow the ways of the world; that is entirely different than someone who has made the choice to live a life pleasing to God and yet slips and sins. Remember: God sees the heart.

- Where's your heart right now? Is there an area of your life that you know you haven't given over to God and are still willfully choosing the way of the world? List your struggle below, and if you feel comfortable, please share this with your group for prayer and accountability.

_____

Now, what about this idea of adultery and that God envies, or as the NASB says "jealously desires." Let's try and gain a better understanding of why James would call the people "adulterous" by reading and summarizing the following verses:

- Jeremiah 2:1-3,20 _____

- Ezekiel 6:9 _____ _____

- Ezekiel 16:32 _____ _____

- Hosea 1:2 _____

- After reading the above verses, why do you think James used the term "adulterous" people" to his readers?

_____

_____

The image being presented is one of spiritual adultery. The nation Israel is pictured as a wandering, faithless wife who turns away from God, her husband, to follow after other gods. Jesus also called the people of His time an "evil and adulterous generation" (Matthew 12:39). Whatever we spend the majority of our time, money, energy and attention on is our "other god."

- What "other god" are you currently serving?_____

When we accept Jesus Christ as our Lord and Savior, we are no longer our own; we were bought at a price (1 Corinthians 6:19-20). We now belong to God, and He doesn't take that lightly.

From the below verses, what promises does God make to us as our spiritual husband?

- Isaiah 55:3 _____

- 2 Timothy 2:13 _____

- Hebrews 13:5 _____

Perhaps these promises seem hard for you to believe because you've had people in your life that have been unfaithful to you. In Hosea 11:9 God says, "...I am God and not man-- the Holy One among you." While others may have been unfaithful to you, God will not and cannot be. Why? Because HE IS GOD, and He cannot lie!

- From James 4:4-5, why do you think God would be envious or jealous?

    _____

    _____

- Summarize God's jealousy in the following verses.

    Exodus 34:14 _____

    Deuteronomy 32:16 _____

    Zechariah 8:2 _____

Zion is just another name for the Jews, God's chosen people. As believers, we are now part of God's chosen people--His bride. Ever found yourself in a situation in your marriage where your spouse began to show special attention to someone of the opposite sex, or maybe someone of the opposite sex started showing special attention to your spouse? Immediately there is a feeling of jealousy because we want to guard what belongs to us, don't we? That's exactly what God thinks as well.

God jealously desires what belongs to Him to stay with Him. When we begin to wander into the things of this world and away from God, He looks to guard our heart from becoming unfaithful to Him. His jealousy is pure and righteous; He seeks what is best for us. The feeling of jealousy is not sin; it's the motive behind the jealousy and how we act out that jealousy that defines whether it is sin.

- Have you ever considered that God gets jealous when you turn away from him to things of the world? (Please discuss)

_____

_____

How has God spoken to you in today's lesson? _____

_____

For the remainder of our lessons this week, James is going to explore the remedy for spiritual adultery--grace. This is no cheap grace, as we will see. It will require action on our part as well, such as submitting to God, resisting the devil, drawing near to God, washing ourselves, mourning and humbling ourselves. As we unwrap some of the various aspects of grace, we are going to find that it's the gift that keeps on giving.

Please read James 4:6-7

- Here's the million dollar question: Define "grace" in your own words.

_____

_____

Not easy to do, is it? As we try to define grace, we begin to see that there are many layers of grace somewhat similar to an onion; as you peel one layer, you begin to see that there are many more layers hiding underneath. Let's start by looking at some of the ways grace is used in the Bible.

Read and summarize grace according to the below verses.

- Romans 5:21 _____

- Romans 6:14 _____

- Ephesians 2:6-7 _____

- Ephesians 2:8 _____

- Ephesians 3:7 _____

- Ephesians 4:7 _____

Grace involves forgiveness, salvation, regeneration, repentance and the love of God. Grace is God's unearned favor and loving-kindness towards us which is evidenced through the influence of His Spirit upon our souls in order to turn us to Jesus, to strengthen us, to increase our faith, knowledge and love, and to ignite within us the desire to grow in likeness to His son, Jesus. Philippians 2:13 says, "...for it is God who works in you to will and to act according to His good purpose." God puts forth His power in us to accomplish His purposes for our life and through our life.

Grace invites us to enter into God's realm; His Spirit moves us and draws us into desiring a relationship with Him by believing in the death of His Son, Jesus Christ, as the substitutional sacrifice for our sins. Believing now brings us into a right relationship with God (righteousness) which allows God's spirit to reign in our lives and calls us to now live under the spirit of His grace rather than our old sin nature. Jesus endows grace to each believer through special talents and qualities that equip us to serve Him. Grace is a gift, plain and simple, and is rich in depth and effect, as you can see.

- How do you see the evidence of God's grace working in your life today?

_____

Review of James 4:1-4.

- What were some of the issues that James was confronting in the church?

_____

_____

After addressing their sinful, selfish hearts, James then says in verse 6, "But He gives us more grace." In our human thinking, it doesn't seem to make sense, does it? Why would God want to give more grace to people who have turned their hearts from Him in selfishness? Answer: BECAUSE HE LOVES US! And He will pour more grace upon us in order to try and draw us back to Him in the hope of reigniting our love for Him and our desire to know, serve and become like Him.

Though grace is a gift, it comes at a high cost--the death of Jesus Christ upon the cross. Therefore, grace also brings responsibility from us.

- What responsibility has God placed on us according to verses 6&7?

_____

_____

We'll talk more about humbling ourselves in day 5, but it's important to note here that God will stand in the way of the proud and will work to hinder and obstruct our prideful agendas. They take us away from Him into an area of believing that we do not need Him and are fully capable and in control without Him. We know that the root behind all pride is the devil who has made himself an enemy of God.

- Is pride keeping you from submitting to God in an area of your life? If so, how?

_____

_____

Verse 6 in the King James version reads, "God resisteth the proud, but giveth grace unto the humble." In verse 7 we're told to resist the devil.

A definition of "resist" is "to withstand the action or effect of;" "to strive against."

- How do you resist the devil in your daily life? _____

  _____

Please read Matthew 4:1-11

- How did Jesus resist the devil?_____

- According to Ephesians 6:10-12, 17, how do we take our stand against the devil's
  schemes?_____

  _____

Do you realize that you are holding in your hands this very moment the most effective weapon we have in resisting the devil? Jesus resisted Satan with God's word, and we are equipped with this same sword in our battle against Satan. God's word has that much power! Wow! Doesn't that just get your adrenaline pumping?

From the following verses, list some additional characteristics of the word of God.

- Psalm 18:30 _____

- Isaiah 40:8 _____

- John 1:1,2&14 _____

- Colossians 1:3-6a _____

- 1 Peter 1:23 _____

- Which verse had the most impact on you? Why? _____

- _____

We will never find fault with God's word because it's flawless; it is living, enduring and stands forever because God stands forever. God's word is truth; it's not a form of truth or "a truth"--it is <u>the truth.</u> Every characteristic applied to God's word is applied to Jesus because He is the Word that became flesh; He is God.

How has God spoken to you in today's lesson? _____

_____

God's word is so exciting! Have you ever had the experience of reading a passage from God's word, and a word or a phrase pops out at you; then a week, month or year later, you read the same passage and a completely different word or phrase pops out at you? You might even have said to yourself that you don't ever remember reading or seeing that passage before. That's because God's word is "living and active" (Hebrews 4:12), and it moves with us in our Christian walk.

Let's jump right in and read today's verses in James 4:8-9

When you willfully sin against God, do you draw closer or pull away from Him? Sin separates us from God, not God from us. Our natural human inclination is to pull away from Him when we willfully sin, isn't it? Our relationship with God is then broken and in need of repair. God's grace convicts us of our sin, but in order for the relationship to be restored, <u>we</u> have to take the first step in drawing near to Him because we must want our relationship with God repaired.

Read Hebrews 4:14-16

-   Why can we approach God's throne of grace with confidence?

    _____

God doesn't bite when we come to Him! Jesus intercedes on our behalf before God's throne because He knows what it's like to be human and tempted; even though He never sinned, He is sympathetic to our weak, sinful nature. He understands. And because He understands, we can draw near to God in full confidence of His understanding heart. Isn't that awesome to know?

After drawing near to God, we're then told to wash our hands, purify our hearts, grieve, mourn and wail. Understanding what James asks is shown with gut-wrenching honesty in the life of King David. **Please turn and read Psalm 51:1-12.**

-   What was David's problem? _____

-   What was his request of God? _____

-   What was his fear? _____

-   What was his desire from God? _____

What a beautiful example this is of a truly humble and repentant heart--one that recognizes their sin and whom they've sinned against and has the desire for forgiveness and cleansing.

- Summarize 2 Chronicles 7:14 _____

_____

James talks about changing our joy to gloom. The Greek word for "gloom" is only found in this one passage in James 4:9 and it means "deep sorrow; to feel miserable." It's the cry of a broken heart. The grief or mourning that James is talking about isn't over a person or a situation, but about our own sin against God.

- (Personal) Have you ever experienced grief over your sin? _____

_____

- What was King David asking of God in Psalm 51:7? _____

In pleading with God to be cleansed, David was literally saying, "Un-sin me." Don't you love it? And what does God have to say about "un-sinning" us from the following?

- Jeremiah 33:8 _____

- Ezekiel 36:25: _____

With all the wonderful promises from God to hear us, forgive and cleanse us, and to sympathize with us in our weaknesses, why on earth do we continue to pull back from God and stay in our sin? Did you know that sin can affect us physically as well as spiritually?

- What do you think David meant in Psalm 51:8? _____

_____

Read Psalm 32:1-5

- Summarize verses 4 & 5 in your own words._____

_____

Have you ever felt depressed to the core in your body with no strength or energy to even get up? A gloom or weight was so heavy upon your soul that you didn't think you could bear it any longer? Did you ever stop to think that it may be a spiritual illness that was showing up physically in you? The gracious hand of God will press down on us in order to draw us to Him for spiritual healing.

-    What was David's remedy according to Psalm 32? _____

In Psalm 51:12, David asks God to restore to him the joy of his salvation. Our spiritual illness lasts only as long as it takes for us to confess and repent of our sin to God. Weeping and mourning won't last forever.

(See Psalm 30:5)

-    What does Jesus promise in Matthew 5:4? _____

"Blessed" means so much more than just being happy because happiness is an emotion that most often depends on the circumstances around us. The blessing that Jesus is talking about is the ultimate spiritual high--the true joy that comes from knowing we belong to God and share in His kingdom. That's the "joy of our salvation."

How has God spoken to you in today's lesson? _____

_____

Humility, humble, humbled - any way you slice it, humility is incompatible with pride; we cannot be full of pride and be humble. Do you remember verse 6 from our lesson in day 3 about pride? "God opposes the proud but gives grace to the humble." God becomes completely free to move in the life of someone who is humble because their humility has invited God in and allowed Him to do His work within them. Someone who is full of pride has limited God's working in their life because they have bought the lie that they're in control of their life, and God is really just there on an as-needed basis when they get into a jam. God said He will "oppose" or stand in the way of this type of attitude in order to get their attention.

Please read James 4:10 along with 1 Peter 5:6.

- What additional things does Peter include?_____

Humility is the result of a heart that has been humbled under the hand of God or through humbling ourselves before God. Unfortunately, any humility we may have gained usually comes from being humbled by God in one way or another since we often tend to be "hard of hearing" when it comes to listening to God and His direction.

- What do you think of when you see a "yield" sign?_____

_____

Have you ever tried to merge onto an interstate and it became apparent that neither you nor the person barreling down on you were willing to yield to one another for the right-of-way because a power game was underway? When we don't yield our hearts to God, we are ultimately playing a power game with Him by saying, "I'm bigger and I'm stronger than you."

Humbling our heart before God means yielding. To yield means to "give over, relinquish, surrender." In essence, you are yielding the right-of-way to God for your life. You won't win the power game, you know. After all, HE IS GOD!

Read Deuteronomy 8:2-3

- What were God's purposes for humbling the Israelites during their 40 years of

  wandering in the desert? _____

_____

God's motive for humbling the Israelites was to test their hearts; in difficulties, would they look for security and fulfillment in what they could see, or would they turn to and depend on God to meet all their needs. Would they fight to be independent of God or realize that their source of life is God.

From the following verses, what promises does God give to those who are humble?

- Psalm 25:9 _____

- Psalm 147:6 _____

God sustains the humble. Do you realize what that really means? Listen to some of the definitions of "sustain." It means to support; bear as a burden; to keep a person from giving way under trials and afflictions; to keep up or keep going; to supply with food, drink and other necessities of life; provide for.

God sustains us physically, emotionally and spiritually. Not only will He help keep us from giving up under trials, but He will support and bear our trials as His burden. He is right by our side whispering, "You can do it." "Keep going." "Don't quit." Also, we won't lack food, clothing and/or shelter, because He provides for our necessities in life. That little word "sustains" says so much, doesn't it?

- We are also told that if we humble ourselves before God, he will lift us up. What do you think it means to be "lifted up" by God?_____

  _____

- Please read the following verses for some additional insight into being lifted up.

  Ezra 9:6 _____

  Job 11:13-15 _____

  Psalm 3:3 _____

Have you ever noticed how a child will hang their head in shame when confronted by a parent over something they have done wrong? They don't want to look mom or dad in the eyes and see their anger, disappointment or even stronger, their hurt.

King David said it beautifully: "...You bestow glory on me and <u>lift up my head</u>." When we humble ourselves before God, recognizing our sin, repenting and confessing it to Him, God lifts up our head saying to us, "Look at me, my child. I love you and I forgive you." What uplifting grace we see in the forgiving eyes of our God.

- What did Jesus invite us to do in Matthew 11:29? _____

_____

Jesus said to "learn from him." He is gentle and humble in heart. Do you want to learn what it looks like to live a life humbly before God? Then study the life of Jesus.

Read Philippians 2:6-11.

- How did Jesus humble himself? _____

- Why was he exalted? _____

- How was he exalted? _____

What did Jesus tell his disciples in Matthew 23:12? _____

_____

Through Jesus' life of obedience and humble dependence on His Father, He was then "exalted to the highest place and given the name that is above every name." Jesus promises us that we, too, will be exalted if we humble ourselves before our Father; the very essence and nature of our character will be raised and elevated before the eyes of God. We have to lose ourselves in God in order to find our true life.

How has God spoken to you in today's lesson? _____

_____

Lesson 9

James 4:11-5:6

Let's jump right into today's verses by reading James 4:11-12.

All of a sudden, we're bouncing back to the law and judgment with a sprinkling of the evils of the tongue thrown in (slander). Are these verses supposed to be summing up everything we've read previously, or does this begin a completely new theme? Perhaps, the best way to look at these verses is as a transitional paragraph connecting the teachings we've already had with the teachings that are to follow through James 5:6, though on a broader scale.

We've all heard the schoolyard chant, "Sticks and stones may break my bones, but words can never hurt me." If only that were true, huh? Sigh.........

- What words have been spoken to you sometime in your life that left a negative impact on you?

_____

_____

Still remember them, don't you? That's because words hurt. No matter how we may try to tell ourselves otherwise, they still hurt.

"You're stupid."   *"You'll never amount to anything."*

"You're clumsy."   *"Try harder." (I'm not satisfied with your results)*

"You're ugly."   *"You're lazy."*

"You're not talented."   *"You're unwanted."*

*You can fill in the blank yourself, can't you? And yet, we continue to think that the hurtful words we say to others won't have the same negative impact on them as hurtful words had on us. It'll be just like water off a duck's back; our hurtful words won't be absorbed into the other person's mind and soul. Worse yet, if you do believe your negative words will have an impact, then the honest truth is that you **want** to hurt someone else with your words for whatever reason.*

- What do you think Jesus means by "careless" in Matthew 12:36? _____

_____

In looking at the Greek word for "careless" (argos), it comes from a root word that means "a negative particle." Listen to some of the other definitions for "careless": unprofitable; lazy; shunning the labor one ought to perform.

The idea here is that watching what we say and choosing our words takes work.

- What does Proverbs 17:27 say about how we are to use our words?

_____

Handcuffs are used to control or hold back someone violent or one who has broken the law. Is there such a thing as tonguecuffs? There are times when we could all use a pair of these, wouldn't you agree? Instead, we must resort to biting our tongue even though it can really, really hurt. The good news is that the hard work of watching our words brings profit (brings benefit and/or yields results). Who does it profit? It profits the person hearing the words you speak.

- According to Proverbs 16:21, how can our pleasant words profit the listener?

_____

What additional things can we learn about restraining our words from the following verses?

- Proverbs 15:23 _____

- Proverbs 29:11 _____

- Ecclesiastes 6:11 _____

- Ecclesiastes 9:17 _____

*A person who knows God has learned how to choose their words with care. They know that to let loose their anger with hurtful words causes them to become out of control and injures the listener. The more words we speak, the less it profits the hearer. At some point they will begin to tune us out, or we will trip over our tongue. Ecclesiastes calls it "the quiet words of the wise." When we take time to make an appropriate reply to someone, we receive joy because we have gained victory over our words by the restraint we've shown through an appropriate response. That means we have to consider our words **before** we speak them out, don't we?*

In James 4:11, he tells us not to slander one another and then immediately describes a slanderer as one who "speaks against his brother or judges him." The Greek word for slander is "katalaleo," and it means "to speak in a harmful manner" about someone or "to defame."

- What does God's law say about slander in Leviticus 19:16? _____

- How do you think we are sitting in judgment of the law when we slander?

_____

One of the definitions of slander is "to defame," which means "to attack the good name or reputation of." If God's law says not to slander and we slander, aren't we then treating God's law as though it were meaningless and attacking His good name in the process? Disregarding God's law slanders the law as beneath our consideration and falsely elevates us to a place where we begin to think we have the right to judge God's law and others. Ouch! Is this spiritual arrogance or what? When we "cherry pick" from God's word on what we like and don't like and on what we will choose to obey and what we won't, aren't we doing the very same thing?

Slander comes from a heart of judgment. We have assessed another person based on words or actions and made a judgment. It doesn't matter that we don't have all the facts, cannot read the other person's heart or that words we may have heard about another person (gossip) are very likely biased and not the complete picture. We judge them anyway.

- Why do you think we find it so difficult to not judge another person's spiritual walk?

   _____

   _____

- How do you struggle in this area? _____

   _____

James reminds us that there is only one Lawgiver and Judge--and it isn't us! Beware of spiritual pride; it's deceitful. Pride operates in an inconspicuous and seemingly harmful way but can have a grave effect. Remember that God will oppose the proud; we are to resist the devil who ultimately is the author of spiritual pride.

How has God spoken to you in today's lesson? _____

   _____

Are you a planner? Do you make short- and long-term plans and then also make backup Plan B and C just in case? If so, then you will relate to today's scripture verses. Even though James is making reference to business plans, we can broaden this idea for our study purposes.

Please read James 4:13-14

- Would you describe yourself as a planner? If so, to what degree? _____
  _____

- When making plans, what types of things do you take into consideration?
  _____

- Read Job 17:11. Can you relate to Job? How do you react when your plans are shattered?
  _____

*Time passes. Our plans don't come to fruition, so we lose heart and give up. Oftentimes, we give up on God or get angry with Him because **our** plans aren't happening in **our** timing and in **our** way. It's funny, though, because we go through our life making plans without God, and then when they don't happen, we blame God. We put God in a lose-lose situation. Even a plan that we think is spiritual like reading the Bible more, as good as it may be, can still be just **our** plan if no interaction with God is tied to it.*

- Have you ever made any spiritual plans? If so, what? _____
  _____

- Do you see your life plans and spiritual plans as separate? _____

We've all heard the term "compartmentalize," I'm sure. It really just means to divide something into categories or compartments. Do you do that with your life plans? Does God fit into the "spiritual" box or compartment while the rest of your life fits elsewhere?

- **Re-read today's verses in James**. What was the issue James was addressing?
  _____

- Do you think it's wrong to make plans for our lives? Please explain. _____
  _____

- What do you learn about planning from the following verses?

  Proverbs 16:3 _____

  Proverbs 16:9 _____

  Proverbs 21:30 _____

So maybe it isn't about making plans for our lives but more about how we go about making those plans. Is God included or isn't He?

- What do you think Paul means by a "worldly manner" in 2 Corinthians 1:17?

  _____

- God addressed this issue as well in Isaiah 30:1. What did he have to say?

  _____

There is a fine line between making plans for our lives and wanting to be in control of our lives. When we go about making plans for our lives as if God doesn't exist, we are ultimately stating to God, "I'm in control of my life, not you." Do we somehow think that by making a Plan A, B and C, we are covering all the perceived variables in a situation and are prepared for whichever one comes about? Do we think that we can somehow control the situation by our detailed planning?

- In making short- and long-term plans for your life, what do you believe is in your control and what is in God's control?

  _____

  _____

Let's take a peek at this issue of control from God's perspective (with more coming tomorrow). What do the following verses have to say about God's control?

- Job 34:13-15 _____

- Jeremiah 31:35 _____

- Colossians 1:15-17 _____

- Hebrews 1:3 _____

While Elihu wasn't always correct in his counsel to Job, in the verses above, he was dead on.

God is in charge of the whole world; it is He who commands the sun, moon and stars to shine. Through the person of Jesus Christ, He has created all things, and He holds everything together by the power of His word alone. Think about it. If He withdrew Himself (His Spirit), everything would fall in on itself, and we would all perish. James asks the question: "What is your life? You are a mist that appears for a little while and then vanishes."

- What additional thoughts does David add in Psalm 39:4-6?

_____

Let's look again at the question that was asked previously. Has your perspective changed at all? Would you answer the question below differently? If so, how?

- In making short- and long-term plans for your life, what do you believe is in your control and what is in God's control?

_____

_____

The desire is strong within us for control over our lives and our destiny. It was the ultimate struggle Adam and Eve had in the Garden--to be independent from God and in control of their lives. It's ironic that we fight so hard for control of something that is a mere pin-dot (a mist, a vapor) when measured against eternity. We're going to continue on this topic more in tomorrow's lesson with regards to God's control, His plans and our presumptions.

How has God spoken to you in today's lesson? _____

_____

Yesterday, we discussed whether it was wrong to make plans for our lives. We came to the conclusion that there is really nothing wrong in making plans and setting goals for our lives, but it's whether or not we invite God into the process and allow Him the opportunity and ability to "shift gears" on us if He so determines. It was made crystal clear to us that ultimately God is in control and in charge of the universe and everything included within (that means us, too)!

Let's go ahead and combine today's verses with those we read yesterday to get a fuller picture of the issue that James was addressing with his readers.

Please re-read James 4:13-14 along with today's verses in 15&16.

- From the context of these verses, about what were the people boasting and bragging?

  _____

  _____

Do you know what it means to presume? The dictionary defines it as excessively forward; impertinent boldness; intrusive. The idea is one of bursting through the door of an area where you have not been invited nor given permission to enter, and then you have the audacity of trying to take charge. The church that James was addressing was boasting and bragging as if they alone were in control of their lives and futures without taking God into consideration in any way, shape or form.

If you're at all familiar with the story of Job, you may remember that in anguish of heart and body he overstepped his boundaries with God. God had a few things to say to Job regarding his presumption that hit Job right between the eyes. But first we need to look at the complaint that Job had made against God.

Read Job 19:6; 21:1-16 & 24:1

- What was Job's complaint against God?_____ _____

  _____

Now let's read God's response in Job chapters 38-39, 40:1-2 & 6-14.

- Briefly summarize in your own words what God was saying to Job.

  _____

  _____

  _____

God called Job out. He said to Job, "Would you discredit my justice? Would you condemn me to justify yourself?" (Job 40:8) In a nutshell He was saying to Job, "Do you no longer consider me deserving of your trust and belief because my justice does not make sense to you? Are you trying to blame me and injure my reputation in order to defend your own sense of right and wrong?"

Ouch! This one hits close to home, doesn't it? How often do we say, "It's not fair." Or how often do we complain that God doesn't love us because we aren't getting our way, or our plans and expectations in life aren't going as we want them to.

- Have you ever been guilty of this? Please share. _____

_____

God clearly didn't mince words with Job. He took him down quite a few notches.

- According to Job 40:3-5 and 42:1-6, how did Job respond God?_____

_____

Job put his hand over his mouth to stop the flow of his words against God. He had a clear understanding that God is God, and he was not! He acknowledged in Job 42:1&2 that God can do all things, and that no plan of God's can be thwarted. So that brings us back around to James 4:15 where James says, "Instead, you ought to say, 'If it is the Lord's will, we will live and do this or that.'"

*One of the questions most frequently asked by Christians is, "How do I find out God's will for my life?" We struggle to determine if we are in His will or out of His will at any given time as if there is one specific road with a sign that says, "God's will straight ahead." And if God would supply a crystal ball so we could see down the road, it would be so much easier to have faith! But Hebrews 11:1 says, "Now faith is being sure of **what we hope for** and certain of what we **do not see**." If we can see it, it's not faith.*

Unfortunately, the future is part of the hidden will of God. Maybe it's not so unfortunate though. If we saw our future before us, not only would we not know how to handle it, we would never be able to fully live in the present.

We search so hard to find out God's will for our lives that in the process we miss the very clear road signs He has put before us about His will. Let's explore the following verses for some direction.

- Micah 6:8 _____

- Deuteronomy 10:12 _____

- John 15:9-10 _____

- Hebrews 11:6 _____

- 2 Peter 3:18 _____

Based on these verses, how would you summarize God's will? _____

_____

Are you catching that it's really more about "being" with God than about "doing" for God? Jesus expressed this very same thing while at the home of his friends Mary and Martha in Luke 10:38-42.

- What do you think was the "one thing needed" that Jesus spoke of in verse 42?

_____

In a loose paraphrase of Matthew 6:33, Jesus tells us to seek first His kingdom and His righteousness, and everything else in life will fall into place and take care of itself. And what does it mean to seek God's kingdom first? It means believing that He exists even though we can't see Him (Hebrews 11); it means getting to know Him by spending time with Him (2 Peter 3); it means not pulling away from Him when we sin (John 15); it means serving Him with our lives (Deuteronomy 10). Simply put, it means "doing life" with God-- walking humbly.

So what about God's plans for our lives? Does being in His will or out of His will affect His plans for us? For that matter, does God really have plans for our individual lives? Well, let's take a look.

- In reading Psalm 32:8, 33:11 and Jeremiah 29:11 what conclusions do you draw?

_____

Isn't it awesome to know that God loves us so intimately that He has plans for our individual lives? And His plans stand firm <u>forever</u>; they are securely fixed in place. However, it's important for us to remember that God's action upon His plans for our lives is directly affected by the degree of obedience to God's will in which we choose to live.

How has God spoken to you in today's lesson? _____

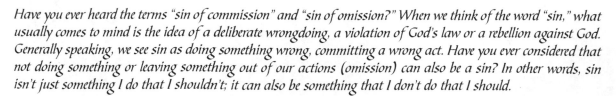

Have you ever heard the terms "sin of commission" and "sin of omission?" When we think of the word "sin," what usually comes to mind is the idea of a deliberate wrongdoing, a violation of God's law or a rebellion against God. Generally speaking, we see sin as doing something wrong, committing a wrong act. Have you ever considered that not doing something or leaving something out of our actions (omission) can also be a sin? In other words, sin isn't just something I do that I shouldn't; it can also be something that I don't do that I should.

Now, before you start to feel trapped by sin, remember Jesus came to redeem us from our sin and forgive us for our sins. Amen and hallelujah! However, as we will see in today's study, sin can be a very personal thing.

Read James 4:17

This seems a bit like a parenthetical verse because while it reminds us that faith without action is really not faith at all, it also serves as a segue into the first part of chapter 5 where James addresses the hoarding of wealth by the rich and their lack of care for others.

- Please summarize verse 17 in your own words. _____

_____

"Anyone, then, who knows the good he ought to do and doesn't do it, sins." Let's look at an example of what this might look like from a woman who shared the following story:

I was on my way to the grocery store one Wednesday afternoon to pick up a few items. On my way into the parking lot, I encountered a homeless man with a sign that simply said: "**Can you help**?"

I had become cynical about how homeless people used the money given to them. I had heard that they would just use the money to buy beer or drugs, so needless to say, I wasn't going to give money to some stranger who was just going to go buy beer anyway. Besides, I reasoned, I gave to my church to help specific organizations with these types of problems.

As I started down the aisle of the grocery store, I heard God speaking to my heart and telling me to give the homeless man $20. No way was I going to give that guy $20 to do who knows what.

As I argued my way up and down the aisles with God, I finally said that I would give him $5 because I didn't know what the money would be used for. God, of course, countered with the original $20 and said something that, to this day, I have never forgotten.

He said, "It doesn't matter what he uses the money for. I have asked you to obey me by giving him $20." As you can guess, my argument with God came to a quick end.

As I got in my car, I rolled down the window, handed the man a $20 bill and told him that God had told me to give him that money. The lesson God taught me that day was that he doesn't always ask the same things from everyone, but he does expect our obedience when he does ask.

Would it be considered a sin for anyone to pass a homeless person and not give them money? Was there a difference in the above situation? Please explain.

_____

_____

According to God's word, circle all of the below that you believe to be biblical sin.

Soap Operas   Body piercings/tattoos   Adultery   Drinking alcohol

Smoking   Lying   Cosmetic surgery   Romance novels

The idea here isn't to debate what is "good or bad" or "right or wrong." While we may all have some of our own personal ideas about biblical sin, in reality, only adultery and lying are addressed as undeniable sins in the Bible. However, for the woman to have not given the homeless man $20 would have been considered a sin before God, because it would have been rebellion against a personal command from God in a particular situation.

Please read 1 Corinthians 6:12 & 9:23.

- What are the similarities? _____

- What are the differences? _____

- What do you think is meant by the expression "Everything is permissible, but not everything is beneficial"?

    _____

    _____

What warning do we receive in Galatians 5:13? _____

_____

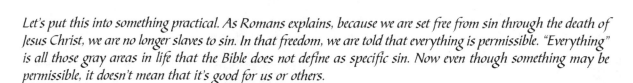

Let's put this into something practical. As Romans explains, because we are set free from sin through the death of Jesus Christ, we are no longer slaves to sin. In that freedom, we are told that everything is permissible. "Everything" is all those gray areas in life that the Bible does not define as specific sin. Now even though something may be permissible, it doesn't mean that it's good for us or others.

Galatians warns us not to use this freedom as a license to sin. That "license" is the green light given to our conscience telling us that something is okay to do because God doesn't say we can't. The reason we are given a warning about our freedom in Christ is because at some point, the very thing we <u>can</u> do in our freedom we now <u>must not do</u> because it controls us (has mastered us). Is a romance novel harmless? Perhaps. Can it master you? Absolutely, as you will see in the following story.

A woman shared that God told her that romance novels had become her god, and she needed to give them up. After some time of struggling in surrender, she asked her husband to bag up all her books and take them to a used book store. As he did this, she tearfully watched realizing for the first time, the importance these books had in her life and the control they had over her.

About two years later, she was reading a book by Billy Graham that talked about God's "permissive" and "perfect" will. She asked God if she could ever read a romance novel again. His reply was that in His permissive will, she could read one now and then, but His perfect will was that she put them away completely.

God loved this woman and <u>knew</u> the control they could potentially have over her. He was gracious in giving her the choice but let her know what His perfect will was on this issue. She had to make the decision as to whether she was mature enough to enter back into this area without being controlled or to stay away altogether. The funny thing is that when she did decide to read a romance novel, it no longer held any appeal for her because God had completely changed her desire through her obedient surrender.

- Has God ever asked you to give up something that had become sin for you? Please share._____

_____

- Is there something you are currently struggling with that you know God is asking you to remove from your life? _____

_____

How has God spoken to you in today's lesson? _____

_____

As a leader of the church in Jerusalem, James wrote this letter to instruct and encourage Christian Jews who had been scattered throughout the nations due to persecution in Jerusalem. Now, in the first six verses of chapter 5, he shifts and begins to address non-Christians. Even though the audience changes from Christians to non-Christians, the subject matter is similar; both James 4:13-17 and 5:1-6 speak of making money and disregarding the will of God.

Read James 5:1-6 and reread 2:6-7

- What are some of the accusations James makes against the wealthy in these verses?

  _____

  _____

- What do you think is the "misery" that will come upon these wealthy people?

  _____

King Solomon came to a realization about riches in Ecclesiastes 5:10-11 & 15-16. Please read and summarize what he had to say.

_____

_____

Perhaps this is where the expression "you can't take it with you" originated. Wealth doesn't last! The riches of this world are not eternal. However, for purposes of a deeper practical application and because we want to make God's word relevant to our everyday lives, let's approach wealth and riches from a different perspective.

According to Dictionary.com, wealth is defined as "a great quantity or store of money, valuable possessions, property or other riches; an abundance of anything, plentiful amount."

Have you ever considered the gifts and talents God has given you as a valuable possession? Hold on! Some of you are already hearing that voice in your head telling you that you don't have any gifts and talents let alone any of value. Put those thoughts on hold, and let's see what God's word has to say about this.

Read and summarize the following verses:

- 1 Corinthians 12:4-6 _____

_____

- 1 Corinthians 12:18-20 _____

_____

- 1 Corinthians 12:27 _____

Are you seeing it? Each and every one of us is a part of the body of Christ (the church), and everyone plays a part in the same way our physical bodies have varying functions.

Please read Romans 12:4-8

- List the various gifts in this passage. _____

_____

Do you see yourself in any of these gifts? What is your passion? Where do your abilities lie? What is your employment? What are your life experiences? All of these things may be an indicator of your gifting from God.

Verse 6 tells us that we all have different gifts "according to the grace given us." God freely gives each believer special gifts to fulfill the various functions (ministries) in the church in order to meet the needs of the body. Our gifts are to be used, not refused. And since we use our gifts by the power of God, there's no basis for thinking that one gift is better or more valuable than any other.

According to the following verses, what is the purpose of our gifts?

- Ephesians 4:11-13 _____

_____

- Ephesians 4:16 _____

Please read 2 Timothy 1:6-7

- What do you think Paul meant when he wrote to Timothy to "*fan into flame the gift of God...*"?

_____

_____

We fan embers, don't we, in order to get a fire going? Our spiritual gifts also come as embers that need to be developed through use. Did you catch that? They are to be **developed through use.** *Sometimes we have to try on a few different areas of ministry to see what fits, but no matter how we slice it, it requires faithful action on our part; we have to be willing to step out in faith and try, believing God has gifted us as part of His body.*

- Verse 7 says, "For God did not give us a spirit of _____ ."

Dictionary.com defines timid as "lacking in self-assurance, courage or bravery; shy; characterized by or indicating fear." Can you relate to any of these definitions personally?

- What keeps you from exploring and using your spiritual gifts? _____

_____

- Do you know your spiritual gift(s)? How are you using them in the body?

_____

_____

Let's look at the encouragement we receive in the second half of verse 7: God gave us "a spirit of power, of love and of self-discipline." There is a two-sided responsibility in this gifting; God's responsibility is to equip us with a specific gift or gifts and empower us to use them with love through His Spirit, and our responsibility is self-discipline.

What does our responsibility look like? Well, are you not serving as part of the body because it cuts into "your time?" Perhaps laziness plays a part as well. Are you afraid of failure or rejection? That's where self-discipline comes in. We must learn to discipline ourselves according to God's word and His promises.

When we see time as belonging to us or we are engulfed in laziness, we are centering our focus on self, so we must discipline ourselves to be God-centered. When we serve in the body using our gifts, God will balance our time and give us the needed energy.

We are told in 1 John 4:18 that "there is no fear in love. But perfect love drives out fear..." Are you holding back from serving in the body because of fear? Fear is not from God but from our enemy, Satan.

Mark 10:45 says: "For even the Son of Man did not come to be served, but to serve, and to give his life as a ransom for many." If Jesus came to serve, can we, as His followers, do anything less?

How has God spoken to you in today's lesson? _____

_____

Notes

Lesson 10

James 5:7-20

The diagnosis of a lack of patience may be a direct result of the toe-tapping society in which we live. Think about it. All life's problems are solved in a 30-minute sitcom; we drive through and can have dinner ready to take home in a mere five minutes. Do you want that new item but don't have the money? No problem. Why wait for what you want when there is credit available at your fingertips. For that matter, do we even need to have patience in today's society?

Patience comes from the Latin word "pati," which means to "suffer, to endure, to bear." It's the ability to endure hardship, misfortune, delay, annoyance, pain etc...without getting angry, frustrated or complaining. I guess that answers the question as to whether we need to have patience in today's society, because most of life's hardships, annoyances, delays, etc. are simply out of our control, aren't they?

Let's read James 5:7-9 together.

In the beginning of chapter five, James was addressing the suffering of Christians by the hands of wealthy non-Christians and their forthcoming judgment from God. In our reading tomorrow, he will address some specific Biblical examples of patience in suffering. In today's verses, James is encouraging us to be patient and stand firm because the Lord will return.

Waiting for anything can seem like a lifetime, but suffering from physical, emotional or spiritual anguish can seem like an eternity, which is why James tells us to stand firm.

- Would you define yourself as a patient person? Please explain. _____
  _____

- Please list the fruit of the spirit from Galatians 5:22-23.
  _____

Did you notice that it doesn't say fruits of the spirit; it's singular--all one fruit. As a Christian, you won't have only joy and peace bestowed upon you while someone else has patience and kindness. If you are a follower of Jesus Christ, you have each one of the virtues listed as fruit of the spirit. Each and every believer has been given the fruit of patience. Now, how that fruit develops is entirely up to you.

- What example of patience did James use in 5:7? _____
- Why do you think he used this example? _____
  _____

When a farmer wants to grow a crop of corn, he starts with a seed which he plants in soil that has been well-prepared. The farmer is dependent on sun, rain and a span of time to help his crop grow--things that are outside of his control. He can check his crop diligently every single day, but he cannot control the rate of growth or when the crop will be ready to harvest. Likewise, the virtue of patience can't be hurried. It is developed slowly over time.

- From Colossians 3:12, what do you think it means to "clothe yourselves" with patience?

_____

_____

Covering ourselves or putting on patience is a deliberate, thought-out action; there is nothing random or haphazard about it. I'm sure we've all heard the lighthearted warning: "Never pray for patience." Why is that? Well, in order for us to develop patience, God must bring circumstances and situations into our life that will test our patience and allow us opportunity to grow and respond with patience. It's sort of a Catch 22, isn't it?

Lifelessons4u has some practical suggestions to help develop patience.

1. Cultivate faith (in God) – Difficulties and tragedies happen to teach and test your faith.

2. Plan ahead - Instead of rushing, give yourself enough time to allow for unforeseen circumstances.

3. Practice acceptance – Sometimes it takes longer to reach your outcome, see changes or be accepted. At times people may disappoint you. It's not what happens that matters, but how you react. Do something constructive while waiting.

4. Take time to help others.

5. Don't rush things.

6. Practice thinking before you speak.

7. Practice delayed gratification.

8. Slow down.

9. Take deep relaxing breaths when you find yourself getting impatient. Whenever we are stressed, we tend to lose our patience (and take it out on others).

Remember, patience takes practice!

- Let's look back at James 5:9 for a minute. Why do you think James warns his readers not to grumble against one another?

  _____

  _____

When we lose our patience, we usually end up taking it out on others by yelling or getting short with them. Maybe that's the grumbling that James is talking about. Impatience can bring out the worst in us if we're not careful.

Let's look at Proverbs 19:11.

From previous lessons, we know that developing Godly wisdom comes from studying God's word and applying it to our lives.

- Discuss how "a man's wisdom gives him patience." _____

  _____

  _____

Do you believe God? Do you take Him at His word? Do you truly believe that He is sovereign and in control of the universe? Understanding and believing this and knowing He is actively involved in our lives, allows us to sit back (have patience) and let God's plan unfold in our lives regardless of what we are going through.

Do you feel like you've been in your current situation for an eternity? Remember that with God, timing is everything! When He acts, He is never late, but rarely is He ever early. Godly wisdom teaches us that God means what He says and says what He means, that His promises are sure and true, and that we can stand firm on His word in any and every situation life throws our way.

How has God spoken to you in today's lesson? _____

_____

Did you come to the conclusion yesterday that you could use a bigger dose of patience in your life in a specific area or areas? Are you feeling impatient for some patience? ☺ Sometimes it feels like it takes forever for spiritual fruit to grow, ripen and mature, doesn't it? Remember, sit back, take a deep breath, relax and remember that God is the best fertilizer to help our fruit ripen and mature.

Please read James 5:10-11

In verse 10, James mentions the suffering of the Lord's servants but doesn't mention any names; however, we can get a sense of some of the suffering they endured just by looking in the book of Hebrews.

- Please read Hebrews 11:32-38 and list some of the suffering the prophets had to endure.

  _____

  _____

We're talking some major physical suffering, aren't we? It would probably be safe to say that most of us have not endured that kind of suffering; however, suffering is a relative thing, is it not? We can always find someone else who is suffering in circumstances much greater than ours, and then we feel guilty for our own feelings. But suffering is personal, individual and comes in various ways and forms.

We've probably all heard the expression "the patience of Job" at one time or another. James talks about patience in suffering and then speaks of Job's perseverance. So was Job patient or did he persevere, or both?

- From yesterday's lesson, what is the definition of patience? _____

  _____

- From Lesson 1, what is the definition of perseverance? _____

  _____

In order for us to make that determination, we're going to have to learn something of Job's life and circumstances.

- Read and summarize Job 1:6-19. _____

  _____

  _____

- How did Job respond in vs. 20-22? _____

- Read and summarize Job 2:1-8 _____

  _____

- How did Job respond in vs. 9-10? _____

Job lost everything--his family, wealth and health. Not to mention, he had a wife who was anything but supportive and encouraging. Through all this, Job accepted that life brings not only good but trouble as well, nor did he blame God for his suffering. Is any of this touching a raw nerve inside of you?

- When you are suffering in difficult circumstances, where do you place blame?

  _____

- What is your expectation of God as a Christian? Do you expect all good and no bad? If so, what happens when you encounter the bad?

  _____

  _____

- So was Job patient? Please read Job 3, 16:1-3 & 21:4 and share your conclusion.

  _____

Patience is a wonderful virtue; it enables us to endure the hardships, delays and annoyances of life without getting angry, frustrated or complaining. Perhaps, patience can be looked at as the attitude we take during life's hardships. Perseverance, on the other hand, is the driving force that keeps us going during difficult times; it is the act of coming to a decision with a fixed purpose or intention--becoming immovable.

- How do you see Job's perseverance reflected in both Job 13:15 and 23:10?

  _____

Jesus shared a short parable regarding attitude and action in Matthew 21:28-32.

- What point was Jesus making in this story? _____

  _____

Patience is the emotional leveler that helps us stay sane during difficulties; however, as the parable showed, God is much more interested in our obedience to Him. Actions do speak louder than words, don't they?

In James 5:11, he states, "As you know, we consider blessed those who have persevered." The Expositor's Bible Commentary, page 267, says, "To be 'blessed' was a common Jewish description connoting wholeness of life and again echoes Jesus' teaching on the upside-down reality in God's kingdom--those who suffer now should be counted as blessed. The path to blessing, therefore, is patient endurance."

- Jesus teaches this concept quite nicely in Matthew 5:11-12. Please read and summarize what he is saying.

_____

_____

Really? Rejoice and be glad when we are insulted, persecuted or slandered? How on earth do we do this? Certainly Jesus wouldn't leave us hanging right here. There must be some "how to" in all this. Absolutely! Verse 11 of James tells us that our Lord is full of compassion and mercy. Because of that, He will not abandon us to figure all this out for ourselves, but He will give us hope, encouragement and direction through His word.

Please read Hebrews 12:-1-11

- What attitude are we called to have?_____

_____

- What action are we called to take? _____

- What encouragement do we receive? _____

_____

- What hope are we given? _____

2 Corinthians 5:7 reminds us, "We live by faith, not by sight."

How has God spoken to you in today's lesson? _____

_____

James is beginning the wind-down to the end of his letter as we can see by the use of the words "above all..." in the beginning of verse 12. He then begins to pack the last few verses with reminders, encouragement and additional principles he still wants to address with his readers.

Let's read James 5:12-16.

We are told in verse 12 not to swear by heaven or by earth or by anything else. The first thing that probably comes to mind when we hear the word "swear" is to think of using profanity or "cussing" by using God's name. Since our desire as Christians is to reflect Jesus Christ in our life and actions, it's pretty clear that using God's name profanely won't reflect the image we are trying to portray; however, what James is addressing here is that of swearing by an oath which simply means to bind ourselves by a vow or pledge.

Is James trying to say it's wrong to take an oath or make a pledge? Legally, we often have to take oaths or make pledges, don't we? Let's turn to the life of Jesus for some direction.

- How did Jesus respond to being charged "under oath" in Matthew 26:62-64?

  _____

- Please read and summarize Jesus teaching in Matthew 5:33-36. _____

  _____

Is this some kind of a contradiction? Jesus tells us not to swear or make an oath, but then when under oath by the high priest, He responds knowing that He is legally obliged to reply. Perhaps, verse 37 can help clear this up.

- Read and compare Matthew 5:37 and the second half of James 5:12.

  _____

- Why do you think people use expressions like, "I swear to God" or "I swear on a stack of Bibles? _____

*What Jesus is speaking about is the idea of meaning what you say and saying what you mean. Are you truthful? Do people believe what you say? When we share an incident or story with someone, and we say something like "I swear to God" or "It's the truth," the implication is that we may not always tell the truth. Because I have ended with the phrase "I swear to God," **this time** I really am telling the truth. It sends a mixed message, doesn't it? Sometimes I tell the truth and sometimes I don't. If my "yes" always means "yes," and my "no" always means "no," then I am known to be sincere in character.*

James moves on to prayer in the next several verses; some of which we will cover today and some tomorrow. Let's take a look at what is being said from an overall perspective rather than a specific word-by-word view. James is trying to get us to understand that we need to turn to God for everything and in everything. Are you in a difficult situation and going through a trial? Are you happy and joyful? Are you suffering from an illness? Have you sinned? Turn to God.

Please read Philippians 4:6-7.

- What keeps you from bringing everything to God in prayer? _____

_____

Think of it this way: Prayer is talking **with God**; *petition is bringing our requests and desires* **to God**; *and thanksgiving is the act of* **praising God**. *As a Christian, prayer is not directed to a "higher power" or some "universal god," but to the Creator of the universe. He invites us to bring everything (needs, hurts, desires, requests) to Him. He yearns for our hearts to be thankful because HE IS GOD; His promises and His word are true and faithful.*

- What promise does verse 7 give us? _____

- Can you share a time when you felt His peace which seemed out of place due to the situation you were in at the time? _____

_____

What do you think 1 Thessalonians 5:17 means when it says to "pray continually?"

_____

Does it seem impossible to you to pray continually? It is possible if we look at prayer not as an action but as an attitude. It's the understanding of what a healthy, vital relationship with God looks like; it requires humility, openness, honesty, consistency and time. Time doesn't have to mean just sitting and reading our Bible, but rather "doing life" with God--walking and talking with Him through the various activities and situations in our lives. Unfortunately, there is a huge obstacle that keeps us from this type of relationship with God. No, it's not time, it's SIN.

In going back to James 5:16, he talks about sickness and healing and then brings sin into the mix. While we don't want to make the assumption that all sickness is related to sin (because we certainly know that isn't the case), we also don't want to rule out the reality that some sickness is related to sin in our lives.

Read and summarize verse 16 in your own words. _____

Is he talking about physical healing or spiritual healing or both? We know that Jesus healed people physically, but He always had a bigger picture in mind when He healed someone.

Please read Matthew 9:1-8.

- According to these verses, why did Jesus heal the paralytic? _____

_____

What did John the Baptist say about Jesus in John 1:29: "Look the _____ _____ _____

who takes away the _____ _____ _____ _____."

Jesus came into the world to forgive and remove sin. For Jesus, it is just as easy to forgive someone of their sin as it is to heal someone who can't walk, and because Jesus loved people and had compassion for their sickness and diseases, He healed them physically. However, by this, Jesus was showing that He had the power not only to heal physically but spiritually as well.

What does 1 John 1:9 say about the forgiveness of sin? _____

James 5:16 tells us to confess our sins to one another and pray for one another in order to be healed.

- If God forgives our sin upon our confession to him, what do you think is the purpose of confessing our sins to one another?

_____

_____

*We've all heard the expression ,"Confession is good for the soul." It's an old Scottish proverb, but it actually says, "**Open** confession is good for the soul." It's the idea of getting something "off your chest." Confessing our personal sin to another allows us to take the secret out of the closet and expose it to the light; it begins to take us out of hiding and back into the mainstream of life. It isn't for the purpose of forgiveness (we've received that in our confession to God), but sometimes we need to acknowledge our sin to a friend, pastor or counselor in order to ask for accountability and receive much needed encouragement and support.*

How has God spoken to you in today's lesson? _____

_____

Yesterday, we purposely left out the second half of verse 16 in order to combine it with today's verses for a better flow. So let's go right into our verses for today.

Please read James 5:16b-18

James strongly states, "The prayer of a righteous man is powerful and effective." He then goes on to back up this statement with an example from the life of Elijah. In order for this example to really benefit us, we'll need to get to know a bit more about Elijah and his life. But in order to do that, we'll need to bring in a bit of Jewish history in order to understand the spiritual and political condition of the Jewish people during Elijah's time.

Abraham, Isaac and Jacob were considered the patriarchs (founders or fathers) of the nation of Israel. It was through their faith in God's promises that God set these people apart for Himself. Jacob had 12 sons who became known as the "Twelve Tribes of Israel." When they settled into the land promised by God, each son received a portion of land named after him as his inheritance.

Many generations later, through the tribe of Judah, King David ruled the nation with righteousness and faith and was considered "a man after God's own heart" (1 Samuel 13:14). When he died, the kingdom was passed to his son Solomon, who ruled with great wisdom. Unfortunately, Solomon in his later years married foreign women who worshipped other gods (see 1 Kings 11). His wives turned his heart toward other gods, so that his heart was no longer fully devoted to the Lord. The result is found in   1 Kings 11:9-13:

> "The Lord became angry with Solomon because his heart had turned away from the Lord, the God of Israel, who had appeared to him twice. Although He had forbidden Solomon to follow other gods, Solomon did not keep the Lord's command. So the Lord said to Solomon, 'Since this is your attitude and you have not kept my covenant and my decrees, which I commanded you, I will most certainly tear the kingdom away from you and give it to one of your subordinates. Nevertheless, for the sake of David your father, I will not do it during your lifetime. I will tear it out of the hand of your son. Yet I will not tear the whole kingdom from him, but will give him one tribe for the sake of David my servant and for the sake of Jerusalem, which I have chosen.'"

When Elijah came into the picture, the nation of Israel had already been divided into 10 northern tribes (knows as Israel) and two southern tribes Judah and Benjamin (known as Judah). Each nation was ruled by a separate king. Elijah lived in Israel under King Ahab. Let's find out what kind of a king he was.

- Please read 1 Kings 16:29-33 and list at least three things you learn about King
  Ahab. _____

  _____

Now Elijah enters the picture in 1 Kings Chapters 17 & 18. Let's read Chapter 17 first.

- Describe the relationship between God and Elijah in these verses. _____

_____

The Greek word for "effective" is "energeo" which means "to work" or "to be active."

- In what ways did Elijah have an effective and powerful prayer life? _____

_____

Let's see how effective and powerful it truly was by reading 1 Kings Chapter 18.

- List some of the things that stand out to you about Elijah in this chapter.

_____

_____

- What challenge did Elijah give the people in 1 Kings 18:21, and how did they respond?

_____

It appears that the people were waiting to decide whom they would serve based on which "god" appeared to be more powerful. The irony is that Baal was considered the god of fertility and the lord of rain clouds but couldn't seem to produce the much needed rain in the land. (God does have a sense of humor.)

What do you think Jesus meant in his statement in Matthew 12:30? _____

_____

There can be no spiritual fence sitting. We can't decide to follow God on Sundays and then live for the world the rest of the week. Jesus was pretty clear; we are either living for Him or against Him--there is no middle ground.

- What made Elijah's prayer life and relationship with God so powerful?

_____

What keeps your prayer life and relationship with God from being effective and powerful?

_____

Could there be a link between the degree of our commitment to God and the effectiveness of our prayers and the relational intimacy we have with Him?

Jesus had some strong words to the church of Laodicea. We are compelled to look at these words and examine them against our own hearts and lives.

Prayerfully read Revelation 3:14-19.

- What do you think Jesus means by the term "lukewarm?" _____

  _____

- From these verses, what do you think caused them to be lukewarm? _____

  _____

They thought they no longer needed God, didn't they? They had wealth and riches; therefore, they had no need of anything else. They had made the mistake of looking through the glasses of the world and thinking they "had it all" rather than through spiritual glasses. Jesus saw the spiritual reality and called them "wretched, pitiful, poor, blind and naked."

- Where are you spiritually right now? Would you define yourself as hot, cold or

  lukewarm? Please share. _____

  _____

Elijah was a man who put his reputation on the line through his faith in God. He believed and expected God would show Himself real, true and all-powerful. He did not waiver in his belief. And even when he prayed for rain and saw nothing, he made his servant go back seven times to look at the sky. He did not give up! And on the seventh time, the servant came back saying he had seen "a cloud as small as a man's hand." That was enough for Elijah to act upon.

*Remember what James said? "The prayer of a <u>righteous</u> man is powerful and effective." While we know righteousness means being in "right standing" with God, it's so much more than that. We have right standing with God when we accept the sacrifice of Jesus Christ for our sin; however, the greater decision is in how we choose to live our lives before God. When we know that in an area(s) of our lives we aren't living in a way that is pleasing to God, it will hinder our prayer lives because **we** know we're doing something wrong. It will put a wedge between us and God. God doesn't move, but **we** do.*

How has God spoken to you in today's lesson? _____

_____

It's hard to believe that we've come to the last day of the last lesson in James. It's been quite a journey, hasn't it? We have been warned, challenged, encouraged and strengthened by James through the various issues he's addressed in this letter. His reason for doing so is to teach us how to live with other Christians in Godly relationships by living out our faith in our daily lives. James closes this letter with a reminder of the responsibility we have towards one another as Christians.

Let's read James 5:19-20.

The idea of wandering is generally thought of as something unintentional or accidental, not thought out or planned. Dictionary.com gives some descriptive meanings to the word "wander." One meaning is "to stray from a path, place or companion."

- As a Christian what might it look like to wander from the following:

    Path _____

    Place _____

    Companion _____

- In looking back at a time when you strayed from God, what were some of the warning signs you failed to notice before you strayed? _____

    _____

What do the below verses teach us about how to keep from straying?

- Psalm 119:35 _____

- Proverbs 17:24 _____

- Proverbs 19:27 _____

- Hebrews 10:25 _____

If we stay on the path of obedience to God's commands and apply them to our daily lives (keeping wisdom in view), if we continue to listen to God's instruction and His words of knowledge, and if we regularly meet with other Christians (at church, Bible study, small groups, etc.), we WILL NOT wander from the truth. If we remove any one of those, we become in danger of wandering.

**Here's a surefire way not to stray,
In God's word you must obey.
Close your heart and close your ears,
And you may wander many years.**

Wandering from Truth

Another definition for the word "wander" is "to take one direction or another without conscious intent or control." Does that mean when we wander, we're unconscious?? ☺ It appears that when we begin to wander or stray, we have somehow allowed our mind to become disengaged; we've "checked out" so to speak.

Our mind and our will play a dual purpose. Try to think of your mind as control central and your will as the leash; where the mind goes, so go the actions. However, our will is the leash that pulls us back when we begin to step out of God's path. Another name for our will is self-control.

What do the following verses say about our mind?

- Colossians 3:2 _____

- Romans 8:6 _____

- 1 Peter 1:13 _____

- Can you share some practical ways you "*set your minds on things above*" and allow God's spirit to control your mind?

    _____

- 1 Peter 1:13 told us to prepare our minds for action and be self-controlled. What kind of action is he speaking about? (see also 1 Peter 5:8)

    _____

*Hebrews 3:12-13 gives us a clear warning: "See to it, brothers, that none of you has a sinful, unbelieving heart that **turns away** from the living God. But encourage one another daily, as long as it is called today, so that none of you may be hardened by sin's deceitfulness."*

Sin is appealing to our human nature; if it wasn't appealing, it wouldn't be tempting. We wander down the path of temptation and away from God. But sin is deceitful as well; it promises great pleasure but delivers pain, heartache and bondage.

God has given us clear direction on how to stay on His path to keep from wandering, but what about someone you know or someone close to you who is beginning to wander or has wandered into sin's deceitfulness and is trapped? Did you know that we have a responsibility to keep one another from wandering or to help bring them back to the truth? It sounds a bit like that ugly word "confrontation," doesn't it? We think of confronting someone as a negative thing, when in reality, it's just lovingly helping someone face the truth of where their wandering has led them.

What do the following two verses say about confrontation and restoration of another believer?

owever, HowH

- Galatians 6:1 _____

- 2 Timothy 2:25-26 _____

- What key word did you see between these two verses? _____

Galatians says "you who are spiritual should restore him gently." Here's where the lie from Satan comes in. He whispers in our ear, "Who are you to talk to them about their sin when you sin as well." We think we're not "spiritual" enough to lovingly and gently confront another person. That is a lie from the pit of hell! Confronting someone about their sin does not mean that we have our act all together or we have reached the pinnacle of spiritual maturity; it simply means that we love someone enough to want to help them get back on the right path.

- Why do you think Galatians gives us the warning to watch ourselves or we may also be tempted?

  _____

  _____

Read Matthew 7:3-5

At first glance, this may look contradictory to what was said above, and that we actually should have it all together before we talk to another person about their sin. However, Jesus knows our human nature, and that it's so much easier to focus on the wrongdoings of others than it is to focus on ourselves.

Jesus is teaching us to keep perspective and balance. What happens if we don't? Well, as Galatians said, we also may be tempted. We may begin to think that we are better than the person we are confronting because we don't struggle with their particular sin which then causes pride in us. We may begin to let down our own spiritual guard and become ripe for attack from Satan in our own area of weakness (which we haven't been focused on because we've been focused on another person's sin), and we begin to wander away ourselves.

Write out 2 Timothy 2:26 _____

_____

Maybe wandering away from God is a bit like being unconscious after all, because the idea is one of waking up, "coming to their senses" as if they'd been asleep.

If our minds are not focused on spiritual realities, if they are not prepared for action and controlled by the spirit of God, we are in danger of falling into a trap set by Satan who then holds us captive to his will. Listen to the spiritual reality that Moses knew from Hebrews 11:24-27:

"By faith Moses, when he had grown up, refused to be known as the son of Pharaoh's daughter. He chose to be mistreated along with the people of God rather than to enjoy the pleasures of sin for a short time. He regarded disgrace for the sake of Christ as of greater value than the treasures of Egypt, because he was looking ahead to his reward. By faith he left Egypt, not fearing the king's anger; he persevered because he saw him who is invisible."

Wow! These are powerful truths. Sin is only pleasurable for a short time before it begins to control us. Moses persevered because he knew that reality wasn't the things he could see, but the God who is invisible; he kept his mind focused on looking ahead to his eternal reward and not on what was happening in front of him.

We have been taught how to keep from wandering, how to stay on God's path, and how to set our minds on the invisible but eternal things of God. But we can't do it alone; it takes being a part of the Christian community in order to encourage one another and help each other from wandering.

What a blessing it has been to journey together these past few weeks. Our journey with God doesn't stop just because our lessons have come to an end. Each one of us must continue our personal walk with God in order to keep from wandering into sin. Remember, we are not alone! God has given us the power of his Holy Spirit, the truth of His word and a community of believers called the "church" to help us on our journey. Thank you God!

How has God spoken to you in today's lesson? _____

_____

Sources

All definitions are from Dictionary.com LLC, Copyright 2010.

The Website is http://dictionary.reference.com

The Blondin story is used by permission from:

www.associatedcontent.com/article/30339

by Maisah Robinson , PhD., published 5/4/2006

Acknowledgements

Many, many, many thanks to my editor, cheerleader, coach and dear friend, Sharon Palacio who helped me "stay the course" when I wanted to quit. Without the countless hours she put into this project, you would not have this in your hands right now.

A big hug and thanks to my husband, Mark who believed in me, encouraged me and gave me the space I needed to accomplish this monumental task!

Warm thanks also go to Sandee Franklin for giving me the "thumbs up" when I initially started and was unsure of direction. She has "held fast in love" throughout this endeavor.

Finally, I must give thanks to Kristin Williams who continually "nagged" me in love to complete this study. While there were times I wanted to duct tape her mouth shut, her tenacity was much needed and welcomed.

Spiritual Gifts Resources

There are many resources available to help you in determining your spiritual gifts from God. You can take a trip to your local Christian bookstore or online to shop for something that fits your taste in writing styles.

A book that I particularly like is an oldie called, "Discover Your God-given Gifts" by Don and Katie Fortune. (Copyright 1987, Fleming H. Revell Company). There is a spiritual gifts test you can take contained in the book and directions on how to score yourself. Once you have determined your gifting, the authors go into depth on the characteristics of each gift (both strengths and weaknesses). Also, included are other people in the Bible who share your spiritual gifting along with how to "live" your gifts.

When researching online for this book, I found that Amazon (www.amazon.com) carried this book along with two others by the same authors: "Discover Your Children's Gifts" and "Discover your Spouse's Gifts."

If you choose to shop online at something like Amazon, you can just type in "spiritual gifts" and a large number of resources will be offered from a variety of authors. If you want a more personal touch, ask for direction and guidance at your local Christian bookstore.

Always remember that "head knowledge" and "feet knowledge" are two different things: You can **know** your spiritual gifts but never **use** your gifts. Remember what James said about faith and action, *"In the same way, faith by itself, if it is not accompanied by action, is dead."* Once you know your gifts, God expects you to use your gifts for His glory.